AN INTRODUCTION TO CRYPTOCURRENCIES

The Crypto Market Ecosystem has emerged as the most profound application of blockchain technology in finance. This textbook adopts an integrated approach, linking traditional functions of the current financial system (payments, traded assets, fundraising, regulation) with the respective functions in the crypto market, in order to facilitate the reader in their understanding of how this new ecosystem works.

The book walks the reader through the main features of the blockchain technology, the definitions, classifications, and distinct characteristics of cryptocurrencies and tokens, how these are evaluated, how funds are raised in the cryptocurrency ecosystem (ICOs), and what the main regulatory approaches are. The authors have compiled more than 100 sources from different sub-fields of economics, finance, and regulation to create a coherent textbook that provides the reader with a clear and easily understandable picture of the new world of encrypted finance and its applications.

The book is primarily aimed at business and finance students, who already have an understanding of the basic principles of how the financial system works, but also targets a more general readership, by virtue of its broader scope and engaging and accessible tone.

Nikos Daskalakis, PhD, is Assistant Professor in Finance and Accounting in Panteion University, Athens, Greece, and a former member of the Banking Stakeholder Group (BSG) of the European Banking Authority (EBA), the European Crowdfunding Stakeholder Forum (ECSF), and the Financial Services User Group (FSUG) of the European Commission. He is an experienced researcher who has published widely cited articles in numerous top-rated journals, and his scientific interests are on crowdfunding, blockchain applications in finance, and SME's access to finance.

Panagiotis Georgitseas is an Anti-Money Laundering and Combating Financing of Terrorism Analyst in the Compliance Group at Eurobank and a PhD Candidate in the Department of Public Administration in Panteion University of Athens. His prior work experience was in Trade Finance Division (Proton Bank S.A.) and in Payment Systems Department (Eurobank). He is member of the Economic Chamber of Greece and his research interests focus on the Economics of Blockchain and to Cryptocurrencies Ecosystem.

Contemporary Issues in Finance

An Introduction to Cryptocurrencies
The Crypto Market Ecosystem
Nikos Daskalakis and Panagiotis Georgitseas

For more information about this series, please visit www.routledge.com/Contemporary-Issues-in-Finance/book-series/CONTEMPFIN

AN INTRODUCTION TO CRYPTOCURRENCIES

The Crypto Market Ecosystem

Nikos Daskalakis and Panagiotis Georgitseas

LONDON AND NEW YORK

First published 2020
by Routledge
2 Park Square, Milton Park, Abingdon, Oxon OX14 4RN

and by Routledge
52 Vanderbilt Avenue, New York, NY 10017

Routledge is an imprint of the Taylor & Francis Group, an informa business

© 2020 Nikos Daskalakis and Panagiotis Georgitseas

The right of Nikos Daskalakis and Panagiotis Georgitseas to be identified as authors of this work has been asserted by them in accordance with sections 77 and 78 of the Copyright, Designs and Patents Act 1988.

All rights reserved. No part of this book may be reprinted or reproduced or utilised in any form or by any electronic, mechanical, or other means, now known or hereafter invented, including photocopying and recording, or in any information storage or retrieval system, without permission in writing from the publishers.

Trademark notice: Product or corporate names may be trademarks or registered trademarks, and are used only for identification and explanation without intent to infringe.

British Library Cataloguing-in-Publication Data
A catalogue record for this book is available from the British Library

Library of Congress Cataloging-in-Publication Data
Names: Daskalakis, Nikos, author. | Georgitseas, Panagiotis, author.
Title: An introduction to cryptocurrencies: the crypto market ecosystem / Nikos Daskalakis and Panagiotis Georgitseas.
Description: Abingdon, Oxon; New York, NY: Routledge, 2020. | Series: Contemporary issues in finance | Includes bibliographical references and index.
Identifiers: LCCN 2020006068 (print) | LCCN 2020006069 (ebook)
Subjects: LCSH: Cryptocurrencies. | Blockchains (Databases) | Finance—Technological innovations.
Classification: LCC HG1710 .D37 2020 (print) | LCC HG1710 (ebook) | DDC 332.4—dc23
LC record available at https://lccn.loc.gov/2020006068
LC ebook record available at https://lccn.loc.gov/2020006069

ISBN: 978-0-367-37077-0 (hbk)
ISBN: 978-0-367-37078-7 (pbk)
ISBN: 978-0-429-35258-4 (ebk)

Typeset in Bembo
by codeMantra

Visit the eResources: www.routledge.com/9780367370787

Nikolaos Daskalakis:

To my wife and children, my guiding light for all my recent and future achievements

Panagiotis Georgitseas:

In memory of Stelios Sfakianakis who recently passed away.
Thank you for always being there for me. You shall not be forgotten.

CONTENTS

List of figures   *ix*
List of tables   *x*

1   The new era of encrypted finance   1
   1.1 The traditional financial system and its main counterparts 1
   1.2 The new era of finance: encrypting the financial system 3
   1.3 Introducing the main counterparts of the new encrypted financial system 5

2   The infrastructure: the blockchain technology   9
   2.1 What is blockchain technology? 9
   2.2 How the blockchain technology works 10
   2.3 How blockchain mining works 12
   2.4 Blockchain consensus mechanisms 13
   2.5 Blockchain 2.0: the Ethereum platform 15
   2.6 Smart contracts 16
   2.7 Alternative uses of blockchain technology 17

3   Traded assets: introduction to cryptocurrencies   20
   3.1 Definitions and taxonomy: digital currencies, virtual currencies,
      cryptocurrencies, and tokens 20
   3.2 How cryptocurrency transactions work 24
   3.3 Properties and main characteristics of cryptocurrencies 26
   3.4 Altcoins (alternative cryptocurrencies) 28
   3.5 Trends in the cryptocurrency market 28
   3.6 Stablecoins 31

viii Contents

4 "Tokenomics" and valuation 37
   4.1 Barriers to pricing and valuation 37
   4.2 Token supply and demand model 38
   4.3 Quantity theory of money 40
   4.4 Token economics of utility 42
   4.5 Combining the monetary policies and the economics of utility 42
   4.6 The discounted cash flow model 43
   4.7 Technical analysis 44

5 Fundraising: initial coin offerings 55
   5.1 Defining initial coin offerings 55
   5.2 The road to ICOs 56
   5.3 How ICOs work 58
   5.4 Main features of an ICO 61
   5.5 Tokens 61
   5.6 The importance of white paper in ICOs 62
   5.7 Comparing ICOs with IPOs and crowdfunding 63

6 The regulatory framework 69
   6.1 Introduction 69
   6.2 United States 70
   6.3 Singapore 71
   6.4 Canada 72
   6.5 China and South Korea 72
   6.6 United Kingdom 73
   6.7 Australia 74
   6.8 Switzerland 74
   6.9 Japan 75
   6.10 European Union (EU) 76
   6.11 Comparative analysis and conclusions of regulatory approaches 77

Index *83*

FIGURES

1.1	The financial system	2
1.2	First bitcoin transaction	4
2.1	Centralized, decentralized, and distributed systems	10
2.2	How blockchain works	11
3.1	Types of currencies in the digital world	21
3.2	The public and private keys of a digital wallet	25
3.3	Example of a digital transaction	26
3.4	Crypto market shares: January 2019	28
3.5	Crypto market shares: January 2014–2018	29
3.6	Types of stablecoins	32
4.1	Price increase from an increase in demand	39
4.2	Price increase from a decrease in supply	39
4.3	Combined effect of monetary policy and economics of utility	43
4.4	USD-BTC Candlestick Bar Chart: January–August 2019	46
4.5	USD-BTC descending triangle pattern example	48
4.6	Example of MACD	49
4.7	Example of PPO	50
4.8	Example of RSI	51
4.9	Different forms of efficient market hypothesis	52
5.1	Main participants in an ICO	56
5.2	ICO vs. VC funding: 2015–2017	57
5.3	Ten most important ICOs during 2013–2018	57
5.4	Number of ICOs and total funds raised: 2017 and 2018	58
5.5	Main steps in an ICO	59
5.6	Fundraising in parallel with token release	60
5.7	Fundraising prior to token release	60

TABLES

3.1	Market caps, market shares, and prices of top eight cryptocurrencies per year	30
3.2	Examples of stablecoins per type	34
5.1	ICOs vs. IPOs	65
5.2	ICOs vs crowdfunding	66
6.1	Regulatory approaches of main jurisdictions	78

1

THE NEW ERA OF ENCRYPTED FINANCE

1.1 The traditional financial system and its main counterparts

A broad definition of the "financial system" is that it is a set of interrelated activities or services structured to facilitate the flow of funds from where they stand to where they are needed. Specifically, for a set period of time, the income of some economic units (households, firms, government) is greater than their expenses, while the income of some others is lower than their expenses. Thus, there must be a way for the funds of the former, surplus economic units to flow to the latter, deficit economic units (Figure 1.1). This is what the financial infrastructure does; it facilitates this flow of funds from where they stand to where they are needed.

This financial infrastructure consists of two main parts: the financial markets (direct finance) and the financial intermediaries (indirect finance). In direct financing, lenders (savers) channel their funds directly to borrowers (spenders), while in indirect financing, lenders (savers) channel their funds to an intermediary, which then decides how to allocate the pool of money they have accumulated to borrowers (spenders). Just two simple examples, one per case. When Bob buys ten shares in the primary market of Sea and Sun plc., a listed company in the London Stock Exchange (LSE), he knows that his money is going directly to Sea and Sun plc. When Mary deposits £100 into her account in a bank, this amount of money is pooled with the deposits of millions of other depositors, and it is for the bank to decide to provide a loan to Sea and Sun plc. In both cases, all participants, Bob, Mary, and Sea and Sun plc. use the infrastructure of a financial market or financial intermediary, respectively, but Bob knows exactly where his money is going (direct finance), while Mary does not (indirect finance). There are plenty of other differences between these two main parts of the financial infrastructure, but this is the broad picture.

2 The new era of encrypted finance

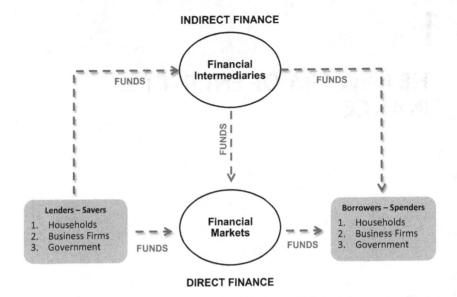

FIGURE 1.1 The financial system.

For a financial system to function properly, there has to be trust in the system. In fact, "a sufficient level of trust" is a necessary precondition for the stability and maintenance of any social, political, and economic system. When trust breaks down, the social system is threatened with unrest, and this is particularly true for the market-based economy, of which the financial system is a part. The notion of trust is of such high importance in finance that if trust is lost, the entire system might collapse, giving rise to what is known as "systemic risk", a type of risk that is widely referred to in finance, especially in the aftermath of the Global Financial Crisis of 2008.

Turning to the basic functions of the financial system, the core objective, as already mentioned above, is to facilitate the allocation and deployment of economic resources, both spatially and across time, in an uncertain environment. This objective can be fulfilled via an efficient payment system, through which all transactions are cleared. The payment system is a core function of the financial system, alongside markets and institutions. Payment, clearing, and settlement arrangements are of fundamental importance for the functioning of the financial system and the conduct of transactions between economic agents in the wider economy. All economic units need to have effective and convenient means of making and receiving payments. Banks and other financial institutions are the primary providers of payment and financial services to end users, as well as being major participants in financial markets and important owners and users of systems for the processing, clearing, and settlement of funds and financial instruments.

Other, subsequent, but equally important, functions are those of: (a) fundraising, where capital is raised for economic units that need it, (b) finance pooling, where small amounts of capital are transformed into larger amounts of funding, (c) liquidity transformation, where the short-term investors'/savers' horizon is transformed to long-term funding for fundraisers, (d) cost reduction, due to the large volume of repeated transactions, (e) risk pooling, which is the practice of sharing risks among a group of other companies, and (f) information and advice providers because of their expertise in the field of finance.

All these functions are carefully embedded in the way the financial infrastructure is developed. Trust is a necessary precondition for the entire system to function properly, while the payment system is a horizontal service that can be seen as the circulatory system of the financial infrastructure. Over time, technology has been constantly creating innovations of how the infrastructure evolves and how the notions of trust and payments can be facilitated, so that the efficiency of the entire system is improved. The most recent innovation that disrupts the way this infrastructure works is the blockchain technology, which is the core technological application in the new era of encrypted finance.

1.2 The new era of finance: encrypting the financial system

The previous section described the basics of the traditional financial system, briefly summarizing the main counterparts, participants, and functions thereof. This section explores how the recent technological innovation of blockchain has already started introducing new and more efficient ways to facilitate certain processes that the financial system currently offers.

It all started back in 2008, when an unknown person or group of people, using the name Satoshi Nakamoto, invented bitcoin. In October 2008, Satoshi Nakamoto published a white paper titled "Bitcoin: A Peer-to-Peer Electronic Cash System"[1] describing bitcoin as "a purely peer-to-peer version of electronic cash, that would allow online payments to be sent directly from one party to another without going through a financial institution". It is worth mentioning that the idea of having a digital currency was already a three-decade-old idea by 2008. From David Chaum's "ecash" in the early 1980s to Wei Dai's "B-money" and Nick Szabo's "Bit Gold" in 1998, this idea was already there. But the main issue of all these early efforts was the double-spending problem, namely, how to make sure that a digital asset is only used once, and how a system can be designed to prevent copying and counterfeiting it. Satoshi Nakamoto's idea of a peer-to-peer electronic cash system, based on the blockchain technology, provided answers to these problems. So, on 3 January 2009, Satoshi Nakamoto mined the Genesis Block, the first mined block in Bitcoin (Figure 1.2), and a new era of encrypted finance began.

The idea of transacting values without the need of a financial institution is a truly disruptive idea for the financial system. The previous section underlined the importance of "trust" as a fundamental prerequisite for the financial system to function without problems. Note that in the absence of trust, the financial system faces systemic risk, that the whole system (not just one participant of the

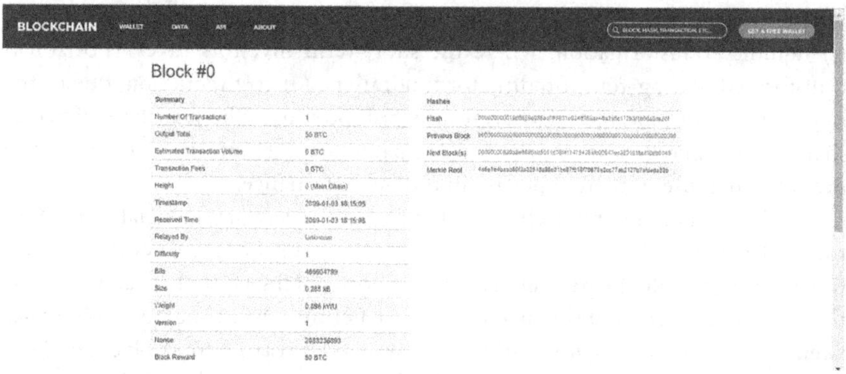

4 The new era of encrypted finance

FIGURE 1.2 First bitcoin transaction.

system) might collapse. Financial institutions also make sure that all transactions are recorded in a way that the double-spending problem is eliminated. So, anything that could emerge to challenge the way transactions services work should fulfill the main prerequisites of trust and double-spending avoidance. Satoshi Nakamoto's idea to create a cryptocurrency using the blockchain technology seemed to fulfill these two necessary requirements.

The key idea behind the notion of "encrypted finance" lies in how the blockchain technology works. Although this technology will be explained in more detail in Chapter 2, it is worth referring here to some main functions of the technology. Blockchain technology uses cryptography. Cryptography is the method of disguising (i.e., encrypting) and revealing (i.e., decrypting) information through complex mathematics. This means that the information can only be viewed by the intended recipients and nobody else. Cryptography is used in blockchain in two ways. The first is via algorithms called cryptographic hash functions, which create a chain of hashes and ensure that the order of transactions is preserved. This resembles the function that the financial institutions use to record transactions in, what is called, a ledger. But unlike a centralized ledger held at one bank, blockchain creates the so called "distributed ledgers" system, where the ledger is distributed across many computers, with each computer having the same view of the ledger. The second way cryptography is used in the blockchain technology is to create digital signatures, which are used to ensure the data put on the blockchain is valid. In bitcoin, the digital signatures are used to ensure the correct amount of value is transferred from one bitcoin wallet to another.

This brief description of how the blockchain technology works shows how trust and the avoidance of the double-spending problem are dealt with. Encrypted transactions, which are practically impossible to break, bring trust to the system, while the distributed ledgers system, where all computers have the same view of the ledger, avoids the double-spending problem. So, when people transact using the blockchain technology, they trust the system for the fact that their transaction is recorded and cannot be counterfeited. For example, when

Bob sends one bitcoin to Mary, they both trust that this transaction is valid and recorded, while anyone has access to the ledger that records transactions, thanks to the distributed ledger system, without necessarily knowing who Bob and Mary are.

These key features of the blockchain technology allow transactions to take place without the need of a financial middleman (markets and/or intermediaries). Bearing in mind that the main function of the financial system is to facilitate the flow of funds from lenders to borrowers, as discussed in Section 1.1, now it is worth looking at how certain participants and processes of the traditional system can be replaced via the use of the blockchain technology.

1.3 Introducing the main counterparts of the new encrypted financial system

Markets and banks act as middlemen in the financial system. They run, control, and own the necessary infrastructure needed for the financial processes to take place. The blockchain technology comes to disrupt certain functions that the traditional financial system offers by suggesting new ways of doing (financial) business. This section will briefly introduce what changes the technology seems to bring in the traditional players and parts of the financial system.

The purpose of this last section of Chapter 1 is to link the functions of the traditional financial system to a set of new processes/services/institutions that seem to emerge in the context of the new, encrypted financial system. Drawing direct links between the traditional and the new system aims to facilitate the understanding of how this new system works. Note that the subsections that follow practically offer a summarized context of the respective remaining chapters of the book.

1.3.1 The infrastructure

The infrastructure of recording transactions in a reliable and foolproof way is key to gain trust for the system. From Babylonian records on slabs of clay to the birth of bookkeeping in the 15th century and to the modern computerized programs, the evolution of infrastructure has been an important game-shifting factor. The gradual financialization of the economy that has taken place during the last 40 years has made the process of recording financial transactions, and mainly payments, an important and fundamental process to the financial system. To date, the payments infrastructure is mainly built and used by the markets and banks. As discussed in Section 1.2, blockchain technology questions this paradigm by allowing transactions/payments to occur without the need of financial intermediation. In the new era of encrypted finance, transactions can be recorded using the blockchain technology without the existence of a financial middleman. Chapter 2 briefly introduces how blockchain works and discusses the main recent advancements of this technology.

1.3.2 The traded assets

Once there is trust that the infrastructure works well in recording transactions, a new system may appear that allows this same infrastructure to be used for multiple other purposes. For example, what if a new asset is created, based on this new technology, that can transfer value? And behold the cryptocurrencies. What if the technology can be developed in something like a self-operating computer program that automatically executes when specific conditions are met (smart contracts) that would allow to broaden the applications of the blockchain technology, from being only a peer-to-peer electronic cash system? And behold the Ethereum platform. What if there are ways to avoid the extreme value fluctuations that cryptocurrencies have to create a currency that respects the fundamental principle of being relatively stable to be accepted as a means of payment? And behold "stablecoins". These are just some broad examples of the numerous applications that the blockchain technology allows.

The problem with these assets is that they differ in some fundamental principles when compared to the well-known, traditional financial assets. For example, if we compare shares with cryptocurrencies or with crypto tokens, a fundamental difference is that most cryptocurrencies do not carry company ownership rights. Another difficulty of these traded assets is that the already thousands of cryptocurrencies that currently exist differ inherently in their functions and in what they offer. For example, we know that the premium segment of the Main Market of the London Stock Exchange trades only equity shares and we understand what the term "shares" means. On the other hand, Binance, one of the biggest global cryptocurrency exchanges to date, allows trading hundreds of cryptocurrencies where each has different attributes and does different things. And to make things more complicated, the means of trading is not a "fiat" currency (i.e., pounds, dollars, euros, etc.), but another cryptocurrency; for example, if Bob wants to buy "Steem" cryptocurrency he would first need to exchange his fiat currency (pounds, dollars, euros, etc.) with bitcoins, and then exchange his bitcoins with Steem.

To sum up, there are brand new traded assets in the new encrypted finance world, with fundamental differences from the traditional financial assets (i.e., stocks, bonds, derivatives, etc.). These new assets are traded in global markets, and the main means of trading is not a fiat currency but other cryptocurrencies (such as bitcoin and Ethereum). Chapter 3 introduces the main features of these crypto assets.

1.3.3 "Tokenomics" and valuation

Valuation is the analytical process to determine how much something is worth. There are several approaches in finance to evaluate traditional financial assets, such as technical and fundamental analysis, the comparative ratio analysis, and the discounted cash flow analysis. There are also several models in economics that regard price determination, such as the simple supply and demand model and the economics of utility. Some of these approaches can also be applied to the crypto assets (i.e., supply and demand, technical analysis), but most of the traditional valuation techniques cannot be applied because of the fundamental differences between the crypto and the financial assets. For example, how can we apply fundamental analysis to cryptocurrencies when there are no financial statements to analyze? Cryptocurrencies are not corporations but are rather digital currencies that represent value or assets within a network. Also, the crypto market is still in its infancy, where most projects are still developing, meaning that there is a lack of track record to use.

The fundamental differences between crypto assets and financial assets, the inherent difficulty even to define what cryptocurrencies are, and the lack of track record have resulted in a very blurred picture of how to evaluate crypto assets. In fact, there is no widely accepted valuation technique that can be applied to cryptocurrencies, except perhaps from the techniques used in technical analysis. Researchers are still trying to understand what the main drivers of prices in the crypto market are, but unless the various crypto assets are clearly classified in distinct categories, and unless the projects financed via initial coin offerings (ICOs) develop their final products and services to start creating a track record, we should not expect big steps in the valuation field, as discussed in Chapter 4.

1.3.4 Fundraising

Perhaps the most important function that the financial system offers, at least from an economic perspective, is the allocation of capital. In the traditional system, this is done via issuing new securities in financial markets, such as issuing shares via an initial public offering (IPO) or the subsequent seasoned equity offerings (SEOs), issuing bonds of all kinds (government, corporate, etc.), and providing loans from financial intermediaries. The equivalent of this fundraising process in the crypto market is done via ICOs. Project owners use ICOs to fund their project, via offering "tokens" (conceptually similar to cryptocurrencies, but broader in scope), in exchange for other, main cryptocurrencies (such as bitcoin and Ethereum), which can in turn be exchanged with fiat currencies so that the project can be funded. ICOs resemble IPOs and crowdfunding, but they also have their own features, which are discussed in Chapter 5.

1.3.5 Regulation

The traditional financial sector is one of the heaviest regulated sectors in the economy. Especially in the aftermath of the 2008 Global Financial Crisis, much of the disaster was attributed to the relatively loose regulatory approach, followed by a belief in self-regulation of the financial industry, which proved to be disastrously wrong. In the years that followed, coordinated efforts from international bodies have gradually led to higher global standards in terms of capital adequacy

8 The new era of encrypted finance

and avoidance of misselling practices to fulfil the two major objectives that regulators should look at: financial stability and consumer protection.

These two core objectives are the starting points of regulators globally when it comes to regulating the crypto market ecosystem. A main difference between the traditional system and the crypto market system is that in the case of the former, financial stability has played a more important role than consumer protection, whereas in the crypto market ecosystem, consumer protection leads a head start. However, within consumer protection, which is the common objective for all regulators, the approaches are very different. Some national authorities have adopted a positive approach toward this new type of financial innovation, whereas others have decided to follow a stricter approach, moving as far as to ban certain functions, such as the ICOs.

The common belief is that regulating the new crypto market ecosystem is not an easy task. The previous subsections discussed the fundamental differences between crypto assets and financial assets, not only between the new crypto market ecosystem and the traditional financial system, but within the crypto market system itself. Some of the core questions that regulators are trying to answer are: Are cryptocurrencies financial assets? Do ICOs resemble traditional fundraising practices? Can cryptocurrencies be used for money laundering and if yes how can this be prevented? Chapter 6 explores the regulatory approaches of the main global jurisdictions, focusing mainly on the ICO issue, since fundraising and capital allocation in general is perhaps the most important function that a financial system offers.

Note

1 https://bitcoin.org/bitcoin.pdf.

Bibliography

Leon Zhao, J., Fan, S., and Yan, J. (2016). Overview of Business Innovations and Research Opportunities in Blockchain and Introduction to the Special Issue, *Financial Innovation*, Vol. 2. doi:10.1186/s40854-016-0049-2.

Merton, R. (1990). The Financial System and Economic Performance. *Journal of Financial Services Research*, Vol. 4, pp. 263–300.

Mishkin, F. S., and Eakins, S. G. (2015). "Financial Markets and Institutions, Global Edition 8/E, Pearson" (April 30). Available at: http://catalogue.pearsoned.co.uk/educator/product/Financial-Markets-and-Institutions-Global-Edition/9781292060484.page#dw_resources

Nakamoto, S. (2009). "Bitcoin: A Peer-to-Peer Electronic Cash System." Available at: https://bitcoin.org/bitcoin.pdf

Roth, F. (2009). The Effect of the Financial Crisis on Systemic Trust. *Intereconomics*, Vol. 44, No. 4, pp. 203–208.

2

THE INFRASTRUCTURE

The blockchain technology

2.1 What is blockchain technology?

In conventional networks of digital payments, there is an imperative need for an intermediary (usually a bank), which records the transactions, and thus avoid double spending. There must be a third party who records all transactions and checks that the amount X sent by one person/account to the other will not be spent again. In this context, the existence of a bank and the notion of trust of all parties involved are necessary for this model to function properly.

In 2009, Satoshi Nakamoto makes the first reference to bitcoin and offers a solution to the problem of double spending. A new decentralized peer-to-peer payment system is proposed, where users will be able to make transactions directly among themselves without a third trusted party. This is possible with the use of blockchain technology, which was first introduced as a public, decentralized platform, without the need for intermediaries, to record the bitcoin cryptocurrency.

Cryptocurrencies are virtual currencies that do not have a material form; rather, they are viewed as digital information. In this context, the blockchain network is usually described as an accounting book, a ledger, where all this digital information is stored, and everyone has access to the information contained in this ledger. Imagine the blockchain network as a ledger that records all transactions, but this ledger is not kept by a bank and does not belong to the bank. Instead, it is public, everyone has access to it at any time, and everyone can have a copy of it; at the same time, personal data of the users are not visible, but encrypted. Imagine the blockchain network as a spreadsheet that is not stored in a central computer but in all the computers (called "nodes") of the network. Every amendment on this spreadsheet becomes visible to all users of the network at the same time and is validated only when nodes verify it. The blockchain network is then a digital platform, which uses cryptographic methods for the storage of information, which cannot be falsified or reversed, and where the entire history of the transactions among the users of the network is recorded, validated, stored, and publicly available.

2.2 How the blockchain technology works

2.2.1 The nature of the system

In computer science, a network can be centralized, decentralized, or distributed as shown in Figure 2.1.

The centralized systems are subject to a central authority. The central node retains full control, with all other nodes connected only to it and obliged to comply with its terms and follow its orders. The distributed systems are not subject to any central authority. Every node is part of a network and connected directly with all the other nodes of the network. The decentralized systems resemble the distributed systems in that they are not subject to any central authority. Their difference is that the nodes in the decentralized systems have two levels: the final nodes (shown in light grey) and the secondary nodes (shown in black). The final nodes (light grey nodes) are connected to the secondary nodes (black nodes) and the secondary nodes are connected among themselves, while the final nodes are not connected to each other. So, a decentralized system is a complex system with many central nodes, each of which supervises a lower level system of nodes.

The blockchain technology is a distributed system. All nodes that participate in the network have equal rights and obligations, store the same amount of information, and are all connected to each other. In a blockchain network, everyone can make entries and these entries must be validated by other users to be added to the block. That is why blockchain technology is also described as distributed ledger technology (DLT).

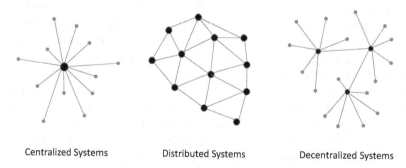

FIGURE 2.1 Centralized, decentralized, and distributed systems.

2.2.2 How it works

Figure 2.2 shows how a transaction in a blockchain occurs using one transaction as an example.[1] Say, Mary wants to send one bitcoin to Bob. Mary logs in her online wallet where she holds her bitcoins. She then picks the amount she wants to send and enters Bob's bitcoin address (which is a series of numbers and letters). She clicks send and a transaction occurs.

This transaction is represented online as a block, which contains encrypted digital information such as the sender and recipient bitcoin addresses and the amount of bitcoin. The block is then broadcast to every party in the network, and, after a process that will be discussed in detail in the next section (the "mining process"), all nodes in the network approve the transaction as valid. Once that happens, the block is added to the chain of the past transactions and Bob receives the bitcoin. Note that every party in the network have their own copy of the ledger, updated with the latest transaction that just took place. Everyone can check the ledger, but no one can modify it.

2.2.3 Safety, transparency, and irreversibility

The way the blockchain works means that there are three main features embedded in the technology: safety, transparency, and irreversibility.

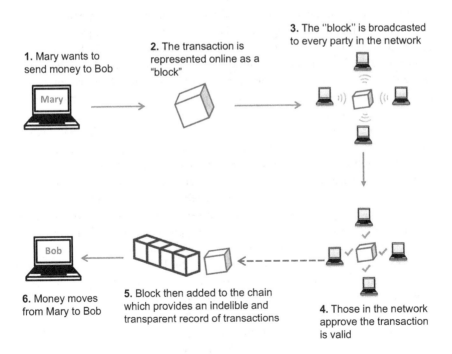

FIGURE 2.2 How blockchain works.

Since every piece of information is stored simultaneously in all computers, it is technically impossible for hackers to change any stored information, as they will have to change it in all computers of the network at the same time. This is the main feature that makes blockchain safe to use.

Since all nodes that participate in the network have equal rights and obligations, all information is publicly stored, displayed, and validated by the whole network, so that no guarantor is required. This makes the system transparent, which is key to create trust in the system.

Last, when a transaction is added to the block, it cannot be amended or deleted. The only way to correct a wrong transaction is for the receiver to pay back the amount to the initial sender so that a new transaction can be re-executed. This irreversibility of the transactions is another important element of this technology.

2.3 How blockchain mining works

Cryptocurrency transactions are performed online, peer-to-peer, and without the involvement of an intermediary. One of the commonest ways that these transactions are verified in blockchain is the so-called "mining" process.[2] Mining is the process followed to add a block in the blockchain, something like the record-keeping service of blockchain. It is a process of common acceptance by all parties in the open network and takes place between Steps 3 and 4 in Figure 2.1.

Miners use specific hardware and software to perform cryptographic calculations, so as to unlock the computational challenges and solve complex algorithms generated by the blockchain system. Once the algorithm is solved, the whole network is informed and the other nodes verify the solution. Once 51% of the miners verify the transaction, the new block is added to the chain. The solution to this complex mathematic algorithm is also the proof of a miner's work. As a reward for the computational power provided, the miner receives a certain amount of the cryptocurrency. This is another major differentiation from the traditional payment systems; transaction costs are either zero, or very low for the parties that transact, as the system itself rewards miners for helping verify the transactions.

This last reward feature creates competition among miners, regarding who will be the first to solve the problem and receive the reward. But mining on its own is a very complex procedure that requires significant computational power and large amounts of energy. As the users of cryptocurrencies and the amount of transactions increase, the mining process becomes more and more demanding, while the more popular the cryptocurrency, the higher the need for an even stronger computational power. In this context, mining popular cryptocurrencies has led to the development of mining farms, which are rooms with a large number of computers and servers that take on tasks of mining. On the other hand, the energy consumption is astonishingly high; for example, the annual energy consumption needed for bitcoin is calculated to be comparable to the annual energy consumption of a 10-million-people country.

Summing up, in a blockchain network, there are nodes and miners. Nodes record the transactions and keep copies of the blockchain, while miners are specialized users who use specific hardware and software to collect the transaction information and validate it. The integrity of the network is maintained by the miners, who are responsible for introducing every new block in the chain. In case miners stop processing the hard-mining process, the whole system might collapse since there will be no way that a transaction can be verified.

2.4 Blockchain consensus mechanisms

The mining process described above is in fact only one, but the most popular to date, of the ways to verify transactions in blockchain and is known as the proof of work (PoW) mechanism. There are a few other transaction verification mechanisms called "consensus mechanisms". They are called so since the blockchain network is a public ledger, so that any update in the ledger (i.e., any new transaction) requires the approval of all the nodes of the network to be valid. A consensus mechanism is a set of rules, commonly accepted by all users in the network, that authorize the system to continue to operate. There are various consensus mechanisms and the choice between them depends on how the project team designs the specific features of each project.

2.4.1 Proof of work (PoW)

The PoW model is the most common consensus mechanism in blockchain. In this model, miners compete to be the first to create the next block of the chain by solving a complex mathematic algorithm. The first one to solve the problem will post the new block with the transactions and receive the reward from the network. The PoW model is often criticized for the huge amount of energy it requires.

2.4.2 Proof of stake (PoS)

An alternative consensus mechanism used in blockchain is the proof of stake (PoS). With PoS, the new block is validated only by those who hold the respective cryptocurrency. A PoS miner is limited to mining a percentage of transactions that is reflective of their ownership stake. For instance, a miner who owns 10% of the available cryptocurrency can theoretically mine only 10% of the blocks. Another difference from PoW is that the validators receive transaction fees as rewards, which are proportional to the number of coins each person holds. The PoS model rewards the investment in the project (the more one invests, the more tokens they generate) and is less decentralized compared to PoW, since it favors those who hold most of the cryptocurrency. On the other hand, PoS uses considerably less energy than PoW and is therefore more cost-efficient.

2.4.3 Delegated proof of stake (DPoS)

The delegated proof of stake (DPoS) is similar to PoS with the difference that not all cryptocurrency holders can be miners. In DPoS, the community votes for specific nodes to act as delegates in the mining process. It was invented by Daniel Larimer and is applied as a consensus mechanism in the EOS cryptocurrency project. In the case of EOS, only 21 elected representatives are responsible for validating transactions. These elected representatives (also called block producers) are voted by the participants in the EOS network, who vote according to the percentage of the digital tokens they hold. Block producers have two roles; they are responsible for mining blocks and for validating transactions, while maintaining the good functioning of the network. For doing so, they receive EOS cryptocurrencies as a reward. In case a block producer remains inactive for 24 hours, they are dismissed and replaced, so that the smooth operation of the network can be maintained. This new method of consensus seems to promote the cooperation among block producers, as opposed to the mining methods that are characterized by competition (as in the case of bitcoin miners). Other important advantages of the DPoS are that less energy consumption is needed and the network is faster. On the other hand, this is a much more centralized system.

2.4.4 Proof of space/capacity

The proof of space/capacity mechanism is very similar to PoW, except that miners do not spend computer power, but they use their hard disk space to mine a block. The more storage space a node provides on their hard disk, the higher the possibility to validate the next block and to receive the reward. PoS works as follows: to verify that a certain amount of hard disk space is reserved for mining, the prover (a node) sends a piece of data to the verifier (usually a member of the project team), who then verifies that the amount of hard disk space is indeed reserved for mining. The node is then entitled to mine blocks and thus receive rewards, via this PoS process. This mechanism requires lower energy consumption than PoW and is therefore seen as a greener alternative to PoW.

2.4.5 Proof of elapsed time (PoET)

The proof of elapsed time (PoET) is an alternative consensus protocol developed by the software company Intel. It works similar to the PoW protocol, but it is more energy efficient. The PoET model is based on the principle of a fair lottery system where every single node is equally likely to be the winner. It spreads the chances of winning fairly across the largest possible number of network participants. The PoET algorithm works as follows. Each node in the blockchain network generates a random wait time and goes to sleep for that specified duration. The one to wake up first – that is, the one with the shortest wait time – wakes up and commits a new block to the blockchain, broadcasting the necessary

The blockchain infrastructure **15**

information to the whole peer network. The same process then is repeated for the creation of the next block.

2.4.6 Proof of importance (PoI)

The proof of importance (PoI) consensus algorithm was first introduced by NEM cryptocurrency project. PoI takes into account one's overall support of the network, like the quantity of the coins a node has, its reputation, its overall activity and the number of transactions it executes. Accounts with a higher importance score will have a higher probability of being chosen to add a block to the blockchain, a process that is known in NEM as "harvesting". In exchange for harvesting a block, nodes are able to collect the transaction fees within that block.

2.4.7 Proof of burn (PoB)

In proof of burn (PoB), miners must show proof that they "burned" some coins, that is they sent the coins to an unspendable address (called an "eater address"), removing them from the circulation permanently. These transactions are recorded in the blockchain, ensuring that there is a necessary proof that the coins cannot be spent again, and the user who burns the coins receives a reward. Essentially, a miner burns their coins to buy a virtual mining right that gives them the power to mine blocks. The more coins burned by the miner, the bigger the virtual mining right. This process does not consume many resources other than the burned coins. This makes the entire mining process energy efficient. The main point of the PoB consensus mechanism is that the user shows a long-term commitment to the coins by burning them, as he suffers a short-term loss in exchange for a long-term profit. The more coins the user burns, the higher their probability to mine the next block. Over time, the user of the PoB continues to receive rewards either by increasing their share or by gaining other benefits in the network.

2.5 Blockchain 2.0: the Ethereum platform

The launch of bitcoin was the first test case of the blockchain technology. This test case proved successful at least in the context of the aims it wished to fulfill, so that people started developing the technology further. A new milestone was reached in 2014 when the Ethereum platform was created by Vitalik Buterin, a Russian-Canadian programmer. At the age of 19, Buterin released a white paper in 2013, describing an alternative platform designed for any type of decentralized application developers would want to build.

This platform allowed the modification of the code that changed the nature of the blocks in the chain, allowing them to create different types of databases, which would be able not only to store a series of additional types of information,

16 The blockchain infrastructure

such as contracts, shares, and even voting results, but also to execute a series of actions, under certain circumstances.

In this new context, project owners can program certain applications that can run on the platform as programmed and can be executed automatically without interruptions or interference by another member. The Ethereum platform is not just a payment system like bitcoin, but a platform designed to allow the development of any decentralized application.

The logic and technology of Ethereum is based on bitcoin, especially in the way it excludes the need of any intermediation to prove and record a transaction. But the Ethereum network emphasizes the following two features: (a) greater speed and higher levels of security of transactions and (b) the efficient operation of different applications other than purely payment systems. It also has its own cryptocurrency, Ether, and anyone who wants to use this platform for an application needs to make use of it.

2.6 Smart contracts

The great innovation of the Ethereum platform is that it allowed to program commands that directly control the transfer of digital currencies or assets between parties under certain conditions. This innovation is called "smart contracts". A smart contract not only defines the rules related to an agreement in the same way that a traditional contract does, but it can also automatically enforce those obligations.

The idea of smart contracts was initially suggested by Szabo,[3] almost two decades before the Ethereum platform was created. Szabo described them as "computer protocols that execute the terms of a contract". They are legal provisions that have been standardized in computing code, so that when they are executed, the relevant agreement is automatically applied. In other words, they are computer protocols that perform, enforce, and verify the execution of the terms of a contract.

Contract terms are introduced in the form of computational commands and are executed through the blockchain technology. By using blockchain technology, they cannot be violated and every contract is recorded in the distributed database. When certain conditions apply, as programmed by the contract terms, then the contract is executed automatically without the interference of intermediaries.

Smart contracts can be designed for anything. A simple example of what smart contracts can do is the case of buying property. Suppose that Bob wishes to buy a piece of property that now belongs to Mary. In real life, he would need to hire a lawyer to check if all papers are legit, he would need to arrange payments with the bank, and he would also need to notify the respective state authority for the purchase. With the use of blockchain technology, the property papers can be uploaded to the blockchain and every single process at the history of the property can be updated so that Bob has a full and clear picture of the history of the property. A smart contract can be designed so that when Bob decides to buy the house and transfers the money, the smart contract is triggered, and, simultaneously, Mary receives the money, property ownership moves to Bob, and the state is informed.

There are already numerous initiatives that explore smart contract technology application in various fields. For example, in the healthcare industry, health records can be kept in a smart contract and stored on the blockchain so that this information can be made available to hospitals and research institutions everywhere. Companies could use smart contracts for any operating expense, such as paying their employees, utility bills, and corporate taxes.

2.7 Alternative uses of blockchain technology

The interest in blockchain technology and in its applications is constantly increasing. Many banks have already started exploring the options offered by this technology, while several public organizations are already looking at the advantages of using blockchain in public services. Two examples, in real estate and the health sectors, have already been mentioned in the previous section, and given below is an indicative list of potential additional applications.

2.7.1 Big data

One of the areas that the blockchain technology could be applied is the management and analysis of Big Data. The blockchain technology can be used to store and distribute data in a secure, fast, easy, and more efficient way.

2.7.2 Public sector

The public sector can use blockchain to automatically tax the executed transactions, since every transaction in blockchain environment would be visible to the public. Also, interesting applications in the health sector have already been discussed in the previous section.

2.7.3 Voting

Another use of this technology is in voting. The technology allows citizens to vote anonymously, avoiding the risk of someone changing the vote, while simultaneously bringing the whole cost for holding elections down.

2.7.4 Tourism industry

Hotel or ticket reservations could be executed automatically with the use of smart contracts without human interference.

18 The blockchain infrastructure

2.7.5 AML and KYC

Anti-money laundering (AML) and know your customer (KYC) details require banks to perform a complex and time-consuming process for each customer. This could be avoided if data is stored on blockchain since the information contained in the blockchain cannot be falsified.

2.7.6 Sharing economy

The sharing economy has a proven success record. Companies like Uber and Airbnb are now widely accepted by the public. Consumers that make use of such sharing services need to rely again on intermediaries like Uber. Blockchain, by allowing peer-to-peer payments, enables direct transactions without the need of an intermediary in this industry.

Notes

1 Note that Figure 2.1 describes just one version of how a blockchain transaction occurs. The technology allows the design of different versions that can offer different ways of transactions validation and control.
2 "Mining" is the most well-known verification process, but the technology allows multiple other ways to verify a transaction as discussed in Section 2.4.
3 Szabo, N. (1997). The Idea of Smart Contracts. Available at: www.fon.hum.uva.nl/ rob/Courses/InformationInSpeech/CDROM/Literature/LOTwinterschool2006/ szabo.best.vwh.net/idea.html.

Bibliography

Cai, Y., and Zhu, D. (2016). Fraud Detections for Online Businesses: A Perspective from Blockchain Technology. *Financial Innovation*. doi:10.1186/s40854-016-0039-4.

Catalini, Christian, and Joshua S. Gans. (2016). "Some Simple Economics of the Blockchain." MIT Sloan Research Paper No. 5191-16.

Christidis, Konstantinos, and Devetsikiotis, Michael. (2016). Blockchains and Smart Contracts for the Internet of Things. *IEEE Access*, Vol. 4, p. 1. doi:10.1109/ACCESS. 2016.2566339.

Condos, James, William H. Sorrell, and Susan L. Donegan. (2016). *Blockchain Technology: Opportunities and Risks*. Office of the Vermont Secretary of State, the Department of Financial Regulation, and the Office of the Attorney General, in consultation with Oliver Goodenough of the Center for Legal Innovation at Vermont Law School, Montpellier, Vermont. Available at: https://legislature.vermont.gov/assets/ Legislative-Reports/blockchain-technology-report-final.pdf

Crosby, M., Pattanayak, P., Verma, S., and Kalyanaraman, V. (2016). Blockchain Technology: Beyond Bitcoin. *Applied Innovation Review*, Vol. 2, pp. 6–10, Sutardja Center for Entrepreneurship and Technology Report, Berkeley University.

De Caria, R. (2017). A Digital Revolution in International Trade? The International Legal Framework for Blockchain Technologies, Virtual Currencies and Smart Contracts: Challenges and Opportunities. In: *Modernizing International Trade Law to Support Innovation and Sustainable Development. UNCITRAL 50th Anniversary* Congress (pp. 1–18). Academic Press, Vienna.

Hegadekatti, Kartik (2016). Analysis of Contracts in Various Formats of Blockchain. *Contracts & Commercial Law eJournal*, Vol. 18, No. 12 (1 March 2017). Available at: https://mpra.ub.uni-muenchen.de/82868/

Jaag, C., and Bach, C. (2017). Blockchain Technology and Cryptocurrencies: Opportunities for Postal Financial Services. In: Crew, M., Parcu, P., and Brennan, T. (eds) *The Changing Postal and Delivery Sector. Topics in Regulatory Economics and Policy*. Working Papers 0056, Swiss Economics. Springer International Publishing Switzerland.

Kakavand, Hossein, Kost De Sevres, Nicolette and Chilton, Bart (2017). The Blockchain Revolution: An Analysis of Regulation and Technology Related to Distributed Ledger Technologies. *SSRN Electronic Journal*. Available at: SSRN: https://ssrn.com/abstract=2849251 or doi: 10.2139/ssrn.2849251.

Kibum Kim, Taewon Kang. (2017). Does Technology against Corruption Always Lead to Benefit? The Potential Risks and Challenges of the Blockchain Technology. *OECD Global Anti-Corruption and Integrity Forum*.

Niforos, Marina, Ramachandran, Vijaya, and Rehermann, Thomas (2017). "Block Chain: Opportunities for Private Enterprises in Emerging Market. International Finance Corporation, Washington, DC." © *International Finance Corporation*. Available at: https://openknowledge.worldbank.org/handle/10986/28962 License: CC BY-NC-ND 3.0 IGO.

Orcutt, Mike (2018, June 14). "EOS's $4 Billion Crypto-Democracy Has Just Launched— And It's Probably Going to be Ruled by Fat Cats." *MIT Technology Review*. Available at: www.technologyreview.com/s/611475/eoss-4-billion-crypto-democracy-has-just-launchedand-its-probably-going-to-be-ruled-by-fat/

Scott, B. (2016). How Can Cryptocurrency and Blockchain Technology Play a Role in Building Social and Solidarity Finance? *United Nations Research Institute for Social Development*.

Swan, M. (2015). *Blockchain: Blueprint for a New Economy*. O'Reilly Media, Inc., Sebastopol, CA.

Szabo, N. (1997). "The Idea of Smart Contracts." Available at: www.fon.hum.uva.nl/rob/Courses/InformationInSpeech/CDROM/Literature/LOTwinterschool2006/szabo.best.vwh.net/idea.html.

Wright, Aaron, and De Filippi, Primavera (2015). Decentralized Blockchain Technology and the Rise of Lex Cryptographia. *SSRN Electronic Journal*. doi:10.2139/ssrn.2580664.

Yingjie, Zhao. (2015). Cryptocurrency Brings New Battles into the Currency Market (March 2015). *Network Architectures and Services*, doi:10.2313/NET-2015-03-1_13.

Yli-Huumo, J., Ko, D., Choi, S., Park, S., and Smolander, K. (2016). Where Is Current Research on Blockchain Technology?—A Systematic Review. *PLOS ONE*, Vol. 11, No. 10, e0163477. doi:10.1371/journal.pone.0163477.

Zheng, Zibin, Xie, Shaoan, Dai, Hong-Ning, Chen, Xiangping, and Wang, Huaimin (2017). An Overview of Blockchain Technology: Architecture, Consensus, and Future Trends. *IEEE International Congress on Big Data*, doi:10.1109/BigDataCongress.2017.85.

3

TRADED ASSETS

Introduction to cryptocurrencies

3.1 Definitions and taxonomy: digital currencies, virtual currencies, cryptocurrencies, and tokens[1]

Defining a new area is not an easy task. It took years before regulators and the industry could agree on defining the different types of crowdfunding, either for the sake of simply communicating or for regulatory purposes. A definition of a new area must be clear enough so that people understand the same thing, but it should also be broad enough to allow the creation of an "area", able to cover a series of different elements that may differ in some features but still share some common characteristics.

The blockchain environment and its applications have given rise to different concepts, difficult to define and categorize. For example, terms like "cryptocurrencies", "virtual currencies", or "digital currencies" are used interchangeably as if they are identical terms, though this is not the case. Something similar holds for "tokens", which are interchangeably used with the term "cryptocurrency", while "tokens" offer a broader range of functions different from "cryptocurrencies".

Figure 3.1 shows the interrelationship of these terms, as approached by the International Monetary Fund (IMF). The graph shows that cryptocurrencies are actually a subcategory of virtual currencies, which in turn are a subcategory of digital currencies. In the paragraphs that follow, an attempt is made to provide the definitions and taxonomy adopted by international organizations so that the features and functions of the elements contained in each category become clearer.

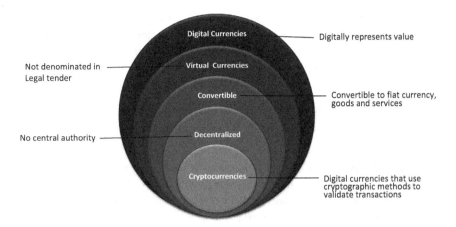

FIGURE 3.1 Types of currencies in the digital world.

3.1.1 Digital currencies

According to the Financial Action Task Force (FATF)[2] "digital currency can mean a digital representation of either virtual currency (non-fiat) or e-money (fiat)". This definition contains the term of "e-money", which is the digital representation of a fiat currency. Since the definition of virtual currency does not include e-money, as will be explained in detail in the next section, digital currencies are, by definition, broader than virtual currencies.

On the other hand, World Bank[3] defines digital currencies as "digital representations of value that are denominated in their own unit of account, distinct from e-money, which is simply a digital payment mechanism, representing and denominated in fiat money", somehow differentiating digital currencies from e-money, although it allows the term *digital payment mechanism* to represent fiat money.

Last, according to the Bank for International Settlements (BIS), digital currencies are "assets represented in digital form" and there are three key aspects related to them. First, they

> typically have some monetary characteristics (such as being used as a means of payment), but are not typically issued in or connected to a sovereign currency, are not a liability of any entity and are not backed by any authority. They have zero intrinsic value and, as a result, they derive value only from the belief that they might be exchanged for other goods or services, or a certain amount of sovereign currency, at a later point in time.

A second key aspect refers to "the way in which these digital currencies are transferred, typically via a built-in distributed ledger". Third, they are issued by

22 Traded assets

a "variety of third-party institutions, almost exclusively non-banks, which have been active in developing and operating digital currency and distributed ledger mechanisms". This last definition is much more descriptive than the first two, and there is an effort to provide certain features to the way they are defined.

3.1.2 Virtual currencies

According to the IMF,[4] virtual currencies are

> digital representations of value, issued by private developers and denominated in their own unit of account. Virtual currencies can be obtained, stored, accessed, and transacted electronically, and can be used for a variety of purposes, as long as the transacting parties agree to use them.

Virtual currencies can be either convertible that allow for the exchange of the virtual currency with fiat currency and for payments for goods and services in the real economy or nonconvertible that operate exclusively within a self-contained virtual environment.

According to the FATF, virtual currency is

> a digital representation of value that can be digitally traded and functions as (1) a medium of exchange; and/or (2) a unit of account; and/or (3) a store of value, but does not have legal tender status (i.e., when tendered to a creditor, is a valid and legal offer of payment) in any jurisdiction.[5]

Since a virtual currency is not issued by any institution that can guarantee its value, its functions are fulfilled only within a virtual community.

Back in 2012, the European Central Bank (ECB) gave the following definition of virtual currencies:[6] "a virtual currency is a type of unregulated, digital money, which is issued and usually controlled by its developers, and used and accepted among the members of a specific virtual community". Three years later[7] the Bank updated the virtual currency definition as "a digital representation of value, not issued by a central bank, credit institution or e-money institution, which in some circumstances can be used as an alternative to money", broadening the scope of use of virtual currencies that could now be used also outside the virtual community. A year later, the ECB highlighted[8] that they "do not qualify as currencies from a Union perspective [and] given that they are not in fact currencies, it would be more accurate to regard them as a means of exchange, rather than as a means of payment".

The ECB classifies virtual currencies into the following three categories:[9]

i   *Closed virtual currency schemes*: These virtual currencies have no link to the real economy and can only be used in online games. Users earn them based on their online performance and the virtual currencies can only be spent within the specific virtual community and cannot be traded outside the virtual community.

ii *Virtual currency schemes with unidirectional flow*: Fiat currencies can be used to buy virtual currencies in this category, but they cannot be exchanged back to fiat currencies. Users can use this kind of virtual currency to purchase virtual goods or services within the community, and sometimes, if allowed, they can redeem them into real goods offered by the community.

iii *Virtual currency schemes with bidirectional flow*: These are virtual currencies that can be traded with fiat currency. They allow for the purchase of both virtual and real goods and services and are similar to any other convertible currency with regard to its interoperability with the real world. The definition of this category best fits with the case of cryptocurrencies.

According to the European Banking Authority (EBA, 2014),[10] a virtual currency is defined as "a digital representation of value that is neither issued by a central bank or public authority […], but is used by natural or legal persons as a means of exchange and can be transferred, stored or traded electronically". The EBA also notes that although some features of virtual currencies resemble the characteristics of electronic money, virtual currencies are not identical to electronic money since the latter is the digital form of the existing fiat currency, which virtual currencies are not.

Last, the US Treasury Department (FinCEN, 2013) defines[11] the virtual currency as "a medium of exchange that operates like a currency in some environments but does not have all the attributes of real currency. In particular, virtual currency does not have legal tender status in any jurisdiction".

Almost all definitions agree on two main things: (a) that virtual currencies are a subset of digital currencies, since they are *digital representations of value* or *digital money*, and (b) that they have *no legal tender status in any jurisdiction*, since they are not issued by a central bank, but by private developers. Some institutions go a bit further in providing specific features that virtual currencies have, such as that they can be *obtained, stored, accessed, and transacted electronically*, or that they *function as a medium of exchange and/or a unit of account and/or a store of value*. Last, another common feature is that jurisdictions refer to the interrelation of virtual currencies with the real world, and how this dimension can categorize them into open or closed systems.

3.1.3 Cryptocurrencies

What differentiates virtual currencies from cryptocurrencies is that the latter term implies the use of cryptography. This is evident in the wording used in a series of policy documents from the institutions referred to in the previous section. For example, the IMF (2016) contrasts virtual currencies and cryptocurrencies as follows: "VC [virtual currency] wallets are used by VC holders to hold and transact in VCs. Cryptocurrencies are stored in digital wallet software associated with cryptographic keys". A report published by the Bank for International Settlement (BIS)[12] clearly mentions that "these [virtual currency] schemes are frequently referred to as 'cryptocurrencies', reflecting the use of cryptography in their issuance, and in the validation of transactions". Last, the World Bank states that "Cryptocurrencies are a subset of digital currencies that rely on cryptographic techniques to achieve consensus".[13]

FATF (2014) defines cryptocurrencies as follows: "Decentralised Virtual Currencies (a.k.a. crypto-currencies) are distributed, open-source, math-based peer-to-peer virtual currencies that have no central administrating authority, and no central monitoring or oversight", while the European Union Agency for Cybersecurity (ENISA) provides the following definition: "Cryptocurrency refers to a math-based, decentralised convertible virtual currency that is protected by cryptography. − i.e., it incorporates principles of cryptography to implement a distributed, decentralised, secure information economy".

Summing up the above definitions, cryptocurrencies are a subset of virtual currencies that use cryptography to operate in a distributed, decentralized, and secure environment.

3.1.4 Tokens

The term "tokens" is not included in Figure 3.1, but it is commonly used interchangeably with the term "cryptocurrencies". This term is also used as a core term in the following chapters, so it is important to define it and explore any differences from "cryptocurrencies".

The European Securities and Markets Authority (ESMA) defines tokens as "any digital representation of an interest, which may be of value, a right to receive a benefit or perform specified functions or may not have a specified purpose or use".[14] According to the ECB, tokens are "mere digital representations of existing assets, which allow recording these assets by means of a different technology".[15]

Both definitions above imply that tokens carry a broader range of functions from "cryptocurrencies", since the latter emphasize on the "currency" concept that they include. Specifically, tokens do share the three main functions of digital currencies and cryptocurrencies mentioned above (medium of exchange; a unit of account; a store of value), but their role is broader and not restricted to being just a "currency". Tokens differ from cryptocurrencies in that they perform more functions than the ones mentioned above. For example, they can provide privileged access to the product or service for which they are issued or even the right to participate in the development of the product/service. This complexity of their functions is also why they are not considered digital currencies and are usually described as digital chips.

3.2 How cryptocurrency transactions work

Cryptocurrencies operate in peer-to-peer networks, with open source protocols. A network with the above technical characteristics is not subject to a central authority and there is no intermediary. The whole network and its transactions are controlled by the users themselves, who are responsible for both confirming the transactions and securing the network.

Cryptocurrencies do not exist in material but only in digital form. The only way to store them is in digital wallets. A digital wallet is a software that sends, receives, and stores digital codes that represent and reflect the value of cryptocurrencies. There are online platforms that offer online digital wallets, but users can also use offline devices that allow them to store their cryptocurrencies offline (hardware wallets). Digital wallets comprise of two keys (Figure 3.2): (a) a public key, which is being used to receive funds; it identifies the individual user's account on the network and it is visible and known to everyone, and (b) a private key, which is only used to sign transactions and prove that the individual user owns the related public key; it is only known by the user and should not be shared.

This pair of public key/private key is generated via a specific encryption algorithm. The two keys are in the form of a string (they contain Latin characters, numbers, and symbols) and have a mathematical relationship between them. Usually, the more characters they contain the greater their security. The symbols and numbers occur randomly after the application of a hash function.[16] These two keys are stored in the user's digital wallet. Each cryptocurrency has its own digital wallet and therefore its own keys. For example, someone who owns three different types of cryptocurrencies will have three different digital wallets with their respective digital keys; note, however, that there already are mixed wallets that allow the storage of more than one cryptocurrencies in one wallet, with different "pockets", namely different public keys.

The owner of a cryptocurrency is the person who owns the private key. This private key is only known to its owner and is the most important element for the operation of the digital wallet. The private key cannot be reissued. If the owner loses the private key, they lose access to their digital wallet and all the cryptocurrencies it contains. The public key on the other hand is the public address of someone's wallet, visible to all users, and where all transactions are being made. But although the public key of the user is publicly visible, it is impossible (technically and computationally) to use it to find the respective private key.

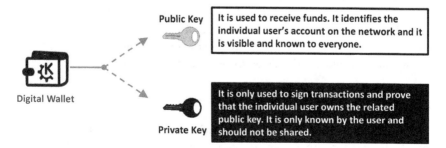

FIGURE 3.2 The public and private keys of a digital wallet.

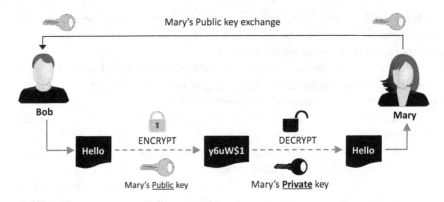

FIGURE 3.3 Example of a digital transaction.

To better understand the key pair function, this could be compared to the function of e-mails. The public key is like the email address that is known to someone who wants to send a message and the private key is like the password of the email account needed to log in and read the message. To give an example of how this pair of key works, suppose that Bob wants to send any type of information (i.e., a message or 1 bitcoin) to Mary (Figure 3.3). Bob uses the public key of Mary (her bitcoin address) to encrypt the digital information of the transaction. Mary then receives the encrypted message and she must use her private key to decrypt it.

3.3 Properties and main characteristics of cryptocurrencies

Cryptocurrencies use the blockchain technology and so they apply the main properties of safety, transparency, and irreversibility that the technology offers. These three and some additional properties of cryptocurrencies are discussed below.

3.3.1 Decentralization

Cryptocurrencies are based on peer-to-peer networks and not on a central server. Transactions are verified by the entire community, the users themselves, and there is no need to rely on a third party. This decentralization feature applies to most cryptocurrencies, but there are exceptions where transactions are verified by either a central authority or a number of delegated participants; the blockchain technology allows these differentiations to exist, and it is up to the designer of the project to decide on the level of decentralization.

3.3.2 Safety

Safety is an inherent feature of the blockchain technology that uses encryption. All transactions are encrypted, and it is practically impossible to hack them and change the chain of transactions. Some concerns were recently raised by advancements in quantum computing, but IT experts believe that blockchain encryption practices can be respectively updated.

3.3.3 Transparency

There are three features of transparency in cryptocurrencies. First, transactions are verified by multiple nodes of the network via a group consensus mechanism. Second, all transactions are recorded in public databases (public ledgers). Third, all users have access to this public record/public ledger at any time.

3.3.4 Irreversibility

The moment a transaction is validated and a block is created and recorded in the blockchain, it cannot be canceled. The only way to reverse a transaction is to create a new one with the opposite direction.

3.3.5 Anonymity

Cryptocurrency transactions are carried out by certifying the digital signatures of the participants and no other personal information is needed. This anonymity feature has raised concerns regarding using the technology for malicious practices (i.e., money laundering and terrorism financing). However, since the entry and exit points to the system (i.e., the exchanges of cryptocurrencies with fiat currencies) can be traced, and since all transactions are recorded and are publicly available in the system, regulators should be able to trace any malicious practices.

3.3.6 Convertibility

All cryptocurrencies are either directly or indirectly convertible with fiat currencies. Some cryptocurrencies (i.e., bitcoin, Ethereum, Litecoin) can be converted directly to fiat currencies. All the others should be first exchanged with the former ones before being cashed out to fiat currencies.

3.3.7 Finite supply

Most cryptocurrencies have a finite supply. Depending on the project, this finite supply can be either exercised from the start, namely produce and offer all tokens, right from the start, or can be gradually reached over time, namely tokens will continue being created via the mining process until a specific supply cap is reached sometime in the future. Note that even though the majority of cryptocurrencies have a finite supply embedded within their protocol, programmers can also create cryptocurrencies that have an infinite supply; the most prominent example here is Ethereum, which has no stated supply cap yet, but this can be introduced by the programmers of the project, if needed.

3.4 Altcoins (alternative cryptocurrencies)

Bitcoin is the first fully decentralized cryptocurrency and perhaps the most popular one, but not the only one. There are currently (August 2019) more than 2,300 cryptocurrencies with a total market value of approximately $330 billion, and a daily transaction volume of $130 billion. The bitcoin still has the largest share of the market, followed by Ethereum and Ripple (Figure 3.4).

All other cryptocurrencies (other than the bitcoin) are called "altcoins" (alternative coins). Most of them appeared since the summer of 2017, mainly due to the meteoric rise of the bitcoin price, which started creating expectations that cryptocurrencies is a rising market which can bring rapid gains. As cryptocurrencies do not fall under any central authority or a specific regulatory framework and everyone can create their own, more and more altcoins started claiming their share in the market, and the market share for altcoins increased from 11.8% in 2014 to 65% in 2018, dropping to 42.4% in January 2019 (Figure 3.5).

Altcoins creators adopted the key features of the blockchain technology and have since tried to either improve these key features (mainly on speed and privacy) or apply this technology in specific business ideas. And while bitcoin and some of the first altcoins were not created as business ideas to create profits, altcoins were mainly created as business projects.

3.5 Trends in the cryptocurrency market

In the first six months of 2017 there was a sudden and tremendous rise in the bitcoin price, from $967.67 at the beginning of 2017 to $19,000 at the end of the same year. This steep rise in bitcoin price contributed to the rise of other

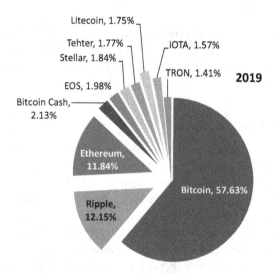

FIGURE 3.4 Crypto market shares: January 2019.

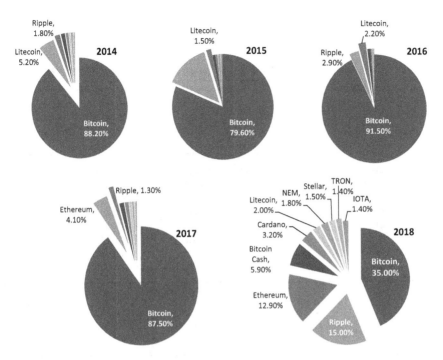

FIGURE 3.5 Crypto market shares: January 2014–2018.

cryptocurrencies. As the bitcoin price kept on rising, investors started looking more at this new market. With the bitcoin price extremely high, many investors turned to the rest of the altcoins with similar expectations of a respective price increase. Similarly, the second largest cryptocurrency, Ethereum, rose from $8.26 at the beginning of 2017 to $1,097 at the end of the year, while Litecoin increased from $4.37 to $300. Table 3.1 shows the capitalization, the market shares, and the price of the eight top cryptocurrencies in the last six years (data from the first week of January of the relevant year).

However, the beginning of 2018 saw the worst first quarter for the value of bitcoin so far. Bitcoin price had fallen to $13,412.44 by the end of January 2018 and to $7,266.07 by the end of March 2018. This extreme downward trend affected the entire coin market by dragging the prices of all other cryptocurrencies down. The fall was further fueled by news of frauds and hacks (such as the $500 million fraud in the Japanese NEM), and this caught the attention of regulators who announced enhanced regulatory audits and interventions. At the same time, banks announced a tougher stance against cryptocurrencies. Lloyds banned their customers from buying bitcoins with their credit cards, while other major banks such as Chase and JPMorgan resorted to similar actions. The most popular social media such as Facebook and Instagram banned cryptocurrency advertisements. Prices were also affected by negative announcements from high-profile institutions, such as the ESMA, which stated that investors risk losing all their capital when investing in cryptocurrencies, since these are highly volatile and are not

30 Traded assets

TABLE 3.1 Market caps, market shares, and prices of top eight cryptocurrencies per year

2014				2015			
Name	*Market cap*	*Market share (%)*	*Price*	*Name*	*Market cap*	*Market share (%)*	*Price*
Bitcoin	$10,543,005,15	88.2	$864.89	Bitcoin	$3,856,201,59	79.6	$281.79
Litecoin	$617,417,99	5.2	$25.13	Ripple	$656,661,64	13.6	$0.02
Ripple	$218,748,69	1.8	$0.03	Litecoin	$74,761,84	1.5	$2.12
Peercoin	$151,559,61	1.3	$7.21	PayCoin	$39,464,54	0.8	$3.2
Omni	$110,190,77	0.9	$177.88	BitShares	$36,149,37	0.7	$0.014
Nxt	$60,503,32	0.5	$0.06	MaidSafe	$21,223,34	0.4	$0.046
Namecoin	$59,406,57	0.5	$7.74	Nxt	$17,361,75	0.4	$0.017
BitShares	$24,970,17	0.2	$19.64	Dogecoin	$16,084,14	0.3	$0.0002

2016				2017			
Name	*Market cap*	*Market share (%)*	*Price*	*Name*	*Market cap*	*Market share (%)*	*Price*
Bitcoin	$6,487,950,80	91.5	$431.45	Bitcoin	$15,482,057,10	87.5	$963.06
Ripple	$202,989,11	2.9	$0.006	Ethereum	$722,829,96	4.1	$8.26
Litecoin	$153,184,84	2.2	$3.49	Ripple	$237,638,34	1.3	$0.0065
Ethereum	$72,409,49	1.0	$0.95	Litecoin	$214,726,27	1.2	$4.37
Dash	$19,820,45	0.3	$3.25	Monero	$185,582,50	1.0	$13.58
Dogecoin	$15,091,78	0.2	$0.00015	Ethereum classic	$127,129,04	0.7	$1.45
Peercoin	$9,788,94	0.1	$0.43	Dash	$78,695,53	0.4	$11.26
BitShares	$8,687,53	0.1	$0.0035	MaidSafeCoin	$44,886,08	0.3	$0.099

2018				2019			
Name	*Market cap*	*Market share (%)*	*Price*	*Name*	*Market cap*	*Market share (%)*	*Price*
Bitcoin	$287,582,315,011	35.0	$17,131	Bitcoin	$63,994.14	57.63	$3,617
Ripple	$123,601,355,156	15.0	$3.19	Ripple	$13,494.08	12.15	$0.3241
Ethereum	$106,276,577,298	12.9	$1,097	Ethereum	$13,143.43	11.84	$121.07
Bitcoin cash	$48,683,234,684	5.9	$2,881	Bitcoin cash	$2,360.14	2.13	$127.37
Cardano	$26,227,470,005	3.2	$1.01	EOS	$2,199.82	1.98	$2.43
Litecoin	$16,400,509,416	2.0	$300	Stellar	$2,042.01	1.84	$0.106
NEM	$15,034,147,365	1.8	$1.67	Tehter	$1,968.63	1.77	$1.00
Stellar	$12,666,677,496	1.5	$0.70	Litecoin	$1,942.86	1.75	$31.09

widely accepted as a means of trading. Last, the bans from China and South Korea also played a key role in the lowering of prices of cryptocurrencies, as very large volumes were traded in these markets. Since the peak of the market at nearly $800 billion in the early days of January 2018 and the bottom that followed at $100 billion in December 2018, the market in 2019 has been fluctuating at around $250 billion.

3.6 Stablecoins

One of the most important features of the term "currency" is the stability of its value. The extreme volatility of the cryptocurrency market has thus defied the very name/title that has been given to this market, that contains the term "currency" in the title. On the other hand, the blockchain technology carries some specific features such as, security, privacy, and transaction costs minimization that could greatly enhance transactions and facilitate payments globally, should the price fluctuation case be dealt with.

In the early 2018, after the sharp rise and fall of the cryptocurrency market, a need for a "stablecoin" was created and these coins started appearing in the market. "Stablecoins" are digital assets (coins or tokens) designed to maintain their value. They do so via a number of different mechanisms, for example, by being pegged to another asset of relatively stable value (i.e., a fiat currency or a commodity), via a process of over-collateralization by other, relatively more stable, cryptos (e.g., Ether, bitcoin), or via algorithmic mechanisms.

Stablecoins share all other features of cryptocurrencies except for volatility. This makes them useful in facilitating transactions in cryptocurrency exchanges and as a means of securing profits from cryptocurrencies trading, but they are not suitable for speculative investments since their valuations are not volatile. Stablecoins can thus be used as a means of payment for daily transactions, as a storage medium, or as a medium of safety when investors expect a drop in the value of crypto markets.

There are three main types of stablecoins (Figure 3.6): (a) fiat-collateralized stablecoins, (b) crypto-collateralized stablecoins, and (c) noncollateralized stablecoins.

3.6.1 Fiat-collateralized stablecoins

This is the simplest and most popular category of stablecoins. The idea is that any issued coin is covered by the equivalent fiat currency, so that each stablecoin has the same value as the corresponding fiat currency. In this case, there is usually a central authority, the coin issuer, who clears transactions (receiving transaction costs) and is responsible for the supply and the liquidation of the coin.

This model works as follows: A depositor deposits a specific amount of the fiat currency (say, US dollars) in an account, the coin issuer company issues the corresponding amount of stablecoins and pays them to the depositor, who is now the stablecoin holder. When the stablecoin holder wishes to liquidate their stablecoins back to the fiat currency, the issuer pays them back the equivalent amount in US dollars and at the same time removes from circulation or destroys the equivalent stablecoins.

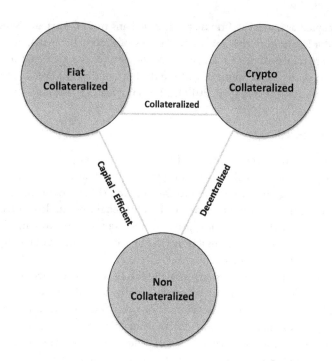

FIGURE 3.6 Types of stablecoins.

For example, say that each "StAble" coin is pegged to $1. Mary deposits $100 to StAble issuer and receives 100 units of the "StAble" cryptocurrency (or 100 StAbles). She can then use her StAble coins to perform any transaction in the crypto ecosystem. If Mary wants to convert her StAbles back to US dollars, she will get back $1 for every StAble coin she converts. Each StAble cryptocurrency is redeemable for $1 so that the ratio between the stablecoin and the fiat currency will always remain at 1:1. So, when the StAble issuer pays back the $100 to Mary, they will have to either destroy or remove 100 StAbles from the circulation.

The main advantage of this type of stablecoins is that the process is simple. Fiat-collateralized stablecoins provide stability as they are backed by fiat currencies, while also maintaining the technological advantages of blockchain. On the other hand, this model requires centralization as there is a need of a coin issuer. So, in this case, regulation is required to regularly check the coin issuer. Another disadvantage is that there are transaction costs, since the issuer will have to be paid for the services they offer and there is no mining process to earn rewards.

Similar to fiat-collateralized stablecoins, some cryptocurrencies are commodity-backed, where holders can redeem their stablecoins at the conversion rate to take possession of commodities.

3.6.2 Crypto-collateralized stablecoins

Crypto-collateralized stablecoins are backed by cryptocurrencies. This brings back the issue of excess volatility in the picture. To avoid this, a process of "over-collateralization" takes place. For example, Bob locks (note here that Bob does not sell/exchange bitcoins; he locks them) bitcoins worth of $100 and receives $50 worth of stablecoins. If the price of the underlying asset (bitcoin here) declines, for example, by 10%, the stablecoin will still keep a stable price, as there will still be a value of $90 in bitcoin backing the value of each stablecoin. This price decline in the underlying asset (not the stablecoin) can go on until a predetermined threshold (say at the level of $75) is reached at which point an auction-type process is triggered where Bob's locked bitcoins are released and offered to the market to cover Bob's loan. This way, the market buys Bob's bitcoins, his loan is settled, and the remaining amount goes back to him. To understand this process better, the institution that issues stablecoins can be viewed as a bank, the stablecoins themselves as loans, and the backing cryptocurrencies as collateral. In reality, Bob receives an overcollateralized loan and when the price of the collateral decreases the institution asks to use collateral to settle the loan.

The advantages of this form of stablecoins are the following: (i) their decentralized structure as opposed to the centralized structure of fiat-collateralized stablecoins; (ii) full transparency since all transactions are recorded in the blockchain; and (iii) fast conversion since stablecoins are easily converted to all other cryptocurrencies. Some of the disadvantages are the following: (i) the underlying assets in this category are cryptocurrencies, which are more unstable than fiat currencies and (ii) the underlying cryptocurrency can be instantly liquidated if its value drops below a certain threshold.

3.6.3 Noncollateralized stablecoins

Noncollateralized stablecoins are not covered by any asset, but they are expected to maintain their value via a controlled supply mechanism. The idea of this concept (developed mainly by Robert Sams, 2014) is to control the monetary supply and therefore the trading price by setting up a smart contract that plays the role of a central bank. Monetary policy here has only one goal: to issue currencies that will maintain their price. In other words, the network burns the coins when the stablecoin price is too low, and issues new coins when the stablecoin price is too high. This function is supported by an algorithm and there is no need for any form of collateral. In fact, the algorithm functions as a central bank, but in a decentralized way, since in traditional systems central banks generally maintain the price stability of fiat currencies with similar mechanisms.

Table 3.2 shows the most important stablecoins of each class.

34 Traded assets

TABLE 3.2 Examples of stablecoins per type

Fiat-collateralized stablecoins	Crypto-collateralized stablecoins	Non-collateralized stablecoins
• TrustToken	• MakerDAO	• Basis
• Tehter	• Havven	• Carbon
• Paxos	• Augmint	• Kowala
• Digix	• Sweetbridge	• Fragments
• Gemini		
• Stably		
• Circle		

Notes

1 The chapter discusses cryptocurrency features that apply to the majority of them. There are exceptions in some features that might differ from the majority, depending on how each project is designed.
2 The Financial Action Task Force (FATF) is an intergovernmental body established in 1989 by the ministers of its member jurisdictions. The objectives of the FATF are to set standards and promote effective implementation of legal, regulatory, and operational measures for combating money laundering, terrorist financing, and other related threats to the integrity of the international financial system.
3 World Bank. (2017). "Distributed Ledger Technology (DLT) and Blockchain." Available at:, http://documents.worldbank.org/curated/en/177911513714062215/pdf/122140-WP-PUBLIC-Distributed-Ledger-Technology-and-Blockchain-Fintech-Notes.pdf.
4 He, Dong, Karl Habermeier, Ross Leckow, Vikram Haksar, Yasmin Almeida, Mikari Kashima, Nadim Kyriakos-Saad, Hiroko Oura, Tahsin Saadi Sedik, Natalia Stetsenko, and Concepcion VerdugoYepes. (2016). "Virtual Currencies and Beyond: Initial Considerations." IMF Staff Discussion Note (January). Available at: www.imf.org/external/pubs/ft/sdn/2016/sdn1603.pdf.
5 FATF. (2014). Virtual Currencies – Key Definitions and Potential AML/CFT Risks, FATF Report, June. Available at: www.fatf-gafi.org/media/fatf/documents/reports/Virtual-currency-key-definitions-and-potential-aml-cft-risks.pdf.
6 European Central Bank. (2012). "Virtual Currencies Schemes." Available at: www.ecb.europa.eu/pub/pdf/other/virtualcurrencyschemes201210en.pdf.
7 European Central Bank. (2015). "Virtual Currency Schemes—A Further Analysis," p. 33. Available at: www.ecb.europa.eu/pub/pdf/other/virtualcurrencyschemesen.pdf.
8 Opinion of the European Central Bank of 12 October 2016 on a proposal for a directive of the European Parliament and of the Council amending Directive (EU) 2015/849 on the prevention of the use of the financial system for the purposes of money laundering or terrorist financing and amending Directive 2009/101/EC, (CON/2016/49), p. 7.
9 European Central Bank. (2012). "Virtual Currencies Schemes." Available at: www.ecb.europa.eu/pub/pdf/other/virtualcurrencyschemes201210en.pdf.
10 European Banking Authority. (2014). "EBA Opinion on 'Virtual Currencies'." EBA/Op/2014/08. Available at: www.eba.europa.eu/documents/10180/657547/EBA-Op-2014-08+Opinion+on+Virtual+Currencies.pdf.
11 U.S. Department of the Treasury. (2013). "Application of FinCEN's Regulations to Persons Administering, Exchanging, or Using Virtual Currencies." (Financial Crimes Enforcement Network, Publication FIN-2013-G001, March 18). Available at: www.fincen.gov/sites/default/files/shared/FIN-2013-G001.pdf.
12 CPMI. (2015). "Digital Currencies" (November). Available at: www.bis.org/cpmi/publ/d137.pdf.

13 World Bank. (2017). "Distributed Ledger Technology (DLT) and Blockchain." Available at: http://documents.worldbank.org/curated/en/177911513714062215/pdf/122140-WP-PUBLIC-Distributed-Ledger-Technology-and-Blockchain-Fintech-Notes.pdf.

14 ESMA. (January 9, 2019). "Advice on Initial Coin Offerings and Crypto-Assets" (January 9). Available at: www.esma.europa.eu/sites/default/files/library/esma50-157-1391_crypto_advice.pdf.

15 ECB. (2019). "Crypto-Assets: Implications for Financial Stability, Monetary Policy, and Payments and Market Infrastructures." ECB Crypto-Assets Task Force, Occasional Paper Series No 233 (May). Available at: www.ecb.europa.eu/pub/pdf/scpops/ecb.op223~3ce14e986c.en.pdf.

16 The hash function in Computer Science is the process in which a mathematical function receives random size data and returns an integral and bit-stable size string.

Bibliography

Ahamad, S., Nair, M., and Varghese, B. (2013). "A Survey on Crypto Currencies." *Proceedings of the International Conference on Advances in Computer Science (AETACS). The 4th International Conference on Advances in Computer Science ACS 2013* (Dec 13–14, 2013 in NCR, India).

Bank for International Settlements (BIS). (2015). "Committee on Payments and Market Infrastructures" (November). *Digital Currencies.* Available at: www.bis.org/cpmi/publ/d137.pdf

"Blockchain: The State of stablecoins. (Report Final)." Available at: www.blockchain.com/ru/static/pdf/StablecoinsReportFinal.pdf

Blundell-Wignall, A. (2014). "The Bitcoin Question: Currency versus Trust-less Transfer Technology." OECD Working Papers on Finance, Insurance and Private Pensions, No. 37, OECD Publishing. doi:10.1787/5jz2pwjd9t20-en.

Brill, Alan, and Keene, Lonnie. (2014). Cryptocurrencies: The Next Generation of Terrorist Financing? *Defence against Terrorism Review*, Vol. 6, No. 1, Spring & Fall, pp. 7–30. Available at: SSRN: https://ssrn.com/abstract=2814914

Dibrova, A. (2016). Virtual Currency: New Step in Monetary Development. *Procedia – Social and Behavioral Sciences*, Vol. 229, pp. 42–49. doi:10.1016/j.sbspro.2016.07.112.

European Banking Authority. (2014). "EBA Opinion on 'Virtual Currencies'." EBA/Op/2014/08. Available at: www.eba.europa.eu/documents/10180/657547/EBA-Op-2014-08+Opinion+on+Virtual+Currencies.pdf.

European Central Bank. (2012). "Virtual Currencies Schemes." Available at: www.ecb.europa.eu/pub/pdf/other/virtualcurrencyschemes201210en.pdf

European Central Bank. (2015). "Virtual Currency Schemes—A Further Analysis," p. 33. Available at: www.ecb.europa.eu/pub/pdf/other/virtualcurrencyschemesen.pdf

ECB. (2016). Opinion of the European Central Bank of October 12, 2016, on a proposal for a directive of the European Parliament and of the Council amending Directive (EU) 2015/849 on the prevention of the use of the financial system for the purposes of money laundering or terrorist financing and amending Directive 2009/101/EC, (CON/2016/49), p. 7.

ENISA Opinion Paper on Cryptocurrencies in the EU. (2017). Available at: www.enisa.europa.eu/publications/enisa-position-papers-and-opinions/enisa-opinion-paper-on-cryptocurrencies-in-the-eu/view

FATF. (2014). "Virtual Currencies Key Definitions and Potential AML/CFT Risks." FATF REPORT (June), p. 4. Available at: www.fatf-gafi.org/media/fatf/documents/reports/Virtual-currency-key-definitions-and-potential-aml-cft-risks.pdf

He, Dong, Karl Habermeier, Ross Leckow, Vikram Haksar, Yasmin Almeida, Mikari Kashima, Nadim Kyriakos-Saad, Hiroko Oura, Tahsin Saadi Sedik, Natalia Stetsenko, and Concepcion VerdugoYepes. (2016). "Virtual Currencies and Beyond: Initial Considerations." IMF Staff Discussion Note (January). Available at: www.imf.org/external/pubs/ft/sdn/2016/sdn1603.pdf

Jaag, C., and Bach, C. (2017). Blockchain Technology and Cryptocurrencies: Opportunities for Postal Financial Services. In: Crew, M., Parcu, P., and Brennan, T. (eds) *The Changing Postal and Delivery Sector. Topics in Regulatory Economics and Policy.* Working Papers 0056, Swiss Economics. Springer International Publishing Switzerland 2017.

Kokes, Josef. (2017). Control Strategy to Trade Cryptocurrencies. *International Journal of Business and Management*, Vol. V, No. 1, pp. 62–69. doi:10.20472/BM.2017.5.1.005.

Kumar, A., and Smith, C. (2017). "Crypto-Currencies – An Introduction to Not-So-Funny Moneys." Reserve Bank of New Zealand Analytical Notes series AN2017/07, Reserve Bank of New Zealand.

Peters, Gareth W., Panayi, Efstathios, and Chapelley, Ariane. (2015). Trends in Cryptocurrencies and Blockchain Technologies: A Monetary Theory and Regulation Perspective. *Journal of Financial Perspectives*, Vol. 3, No. 3, pp. 92–113. https://EconPapers.repec.org/RePEc:ris:jofipe:0089.

Richter, C., Kraus, S., and Bouncken, R. B. (2015). "Virtual Currencies like Bitcoin as a Paradigm Shift in the Field of Transactions." *International Business & Economics Research Journal*, Vol. 14, No. 4, pp. 575–586.

Rose, Chris. (2015). The Evolution of Digital Currencies: Bitcoin, a Cryptocurrency Causing a Monetary Revolution. *International Business & Economics Research Journal (IBER)*, Vol. 14, p. 617. doi:10.19030/iber.v14i4.9353.

Sams, R. (2014). "A Note on Cryptocurrency Stabilisation: Segniorage Shares." Available at: https://assets.ctfassets.net/sdlntm3tthp6/resource-asset-r390/5a940afb21681d-19c0b3b76cf69259e1/58ebe9e2-1f28-4a8d-8ce1-26abef07aedf.pdf

U.S. Department of the Treasury. (2013). "Application of FinCEN's Regulations to Persons Administering, Exchanging, or Using Virtual Currencies." (Financial Crimes Enforcement Network, Publication FIN-2013-G001, March 18, 2013). Available at http://fincen.gov/statutes_regs/guidance/html/FIN-2013-G001.html

White, Lawrence H. (2014). "The Market for Cryptocurrencies." GMU Working Paper in Economics No. 14–45. Available at: SSRN: https://ssrn.com/abstract=2538290 or doi:10.2139/ssrn.2538290.

Yingjie, Zhao. (2015). Cryptocurrency Brings New Battles into the Currency Market (March 2015). *Network Architectures and Services.* doi:10.2313/NET-2015-03-1_13.

4

"TOKENOMICS" AND VALUATION

4.1 Barriers to pricing and valuation

Perhaps the most important problem that investors face in the crypto market to date is the pricing and valuation of cryptocurrencies, tokens, or coins.[1] So far, there are no commonly accepted pricing and valuation models to determine a "fair" value of tokens because the traditional economics and financial valuation models cannot be easily applied. This is mainly because of the broader nature of the traded assets, as discussed in Chapter 3, where some tokens are mainly utility tokens, others have plain currency features (without any fundamentals), while others simply reflect a new technology with unclear business applications yet. So, the definition and categorization of the traded assets are of great importance in creating valuation contexts. For example, if there is a way to categorize some tokens as "security tokens" or "asset tokens", where these tokens can bring future cash flows, and are thus similar to shares, bonds, and derivatives, then it would be easier to apply the traditional valuation techniques. But even in these cases, it seems to be still too early (August 2019) to look at a consistent example of an asset token, whose project has started generating cash flows.

So, the first barrier to valuation is the inherent broadness of the nature of the projects they are linked with and the respective lack of a categorization that would allow testing some traditional valuation methods to a specific set of those (namely the security/asset tokens). The second main barrier when trying to evaluate the traded assets is the lack of track record of fundamental data that could serve as a basis to forecast future flows and apply respective methods such as the discounted cash flow method. This lack of historic fundamental data makes fundamental analysis almost impossible. In this context, comparative analysis should also be excluded since there is no comparable information structured in a commonly acceptable way, such as financial statements of companies.

38 "Tokenomics" and valuation

Another important barrier is that, in most cases, tokens have finite supplies, which encourages people to hold them than to trade them in the secondary market, anticipating higher demand in the future and consequently higher prices. This "hold" strategy is further encouraged by the fact that most projects are still at their very early stages, and token holders are mainly speculators that expect that sometime in the future, the tokens they hold will eventually develop a "true" function that will allow them to sell them to someone who needs them as access to this specific function. Last, the value of a (mainly utility) token is linked with its use in a particular computing network, which is very different from the traditional cash flow generation of a company linked with its share price, which makes valuation even more complicated.

In this complicated context, the purpose of this chapter is to explore the current approaches in token pricing and valuation, bearing in mind the above-mentioned barriers. Various approaches are discussed, ranging from the supply and demand model but focusing on the supply side of the token (token monetary policy), to their utility side (token economics of utility), to their function as a currency (quantity theory of money), and to their features as financial assets (technical and fundamental analysis).

4.2 Token supply and demand model

A simple model of price determination in economics is the supply and demand model. According to the model, the price of an item is viewed as an equilibrium mechanism where supply and demand curves cross. This model can also be applied in the case of tokens. A simple application of the model can be seen in Figures 4.1. and 4.2, where a price increase is explored.

First, note that the supply curves in both graphs are vertical to the quantity axis. This implies that the supply of the token is a predetermined number, not affected by the price of the token. This is the case of the most cryptocurrencies, since the supply of tokens is a finite and predetermined number, already known to the market participants. The way this finite number is allocated in the market may differ from token to token, as will be further discussed in the case of Figure 4.2, but the total supply of tokens to be issued is usually known in advance.

In Figure 4.1 the price of a token increases via an increase in demand, provided that the supply of tokens is stable. This is the predominant approach or expectation in the crypto world for the time being. Most crypto market participants that are not actively trading, expect that the projects whose tokens they hold, will eventually grow to a level where specific products or services can be linked with so that people/entities that would like to make use of these products/services will have to buy the respective tokens so that the demand will increase. Because most tokens have a finite supply, an increase in demand will drive the token price up, as Figure 4.1 shows.

Figure 4.2 describes the case where the demand of a token remains unchanged, but there are changes in the supply of the token. This gives rise to the

"Tokenomics" and valuation **39**

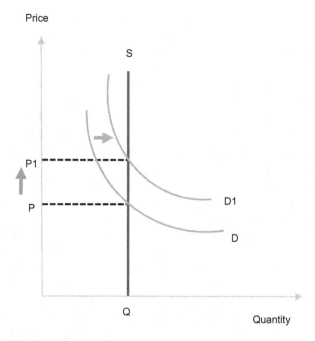

FIGURE 4.1 Price increase from an increase in demand.

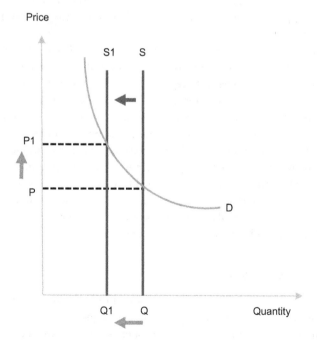

FIGURE 4.2 Price increase from a decrease in supply.

40 "Tokenomics" and valuation

so-called token monetary policy approach, which explains how changes in the supply of the tokens can affect their price. Since the token supply can be directly controlled by the issuer, while the token demand depends on factors that cannot be endogenously controlled, the token monetary policy approach is an area that has attracted much of interest in token economics and is discussed as a central approach of price determination in the cryptocurrency area.

The token monetary policy approach explores how tokens are distributed and more specifically how they are released to the public. There are several different types of monetary models (fixed supply, supply with constant inflation rate, with decaying inflation rate, or with variable rates, algorithmic), and the team behind the project is the one to determine which monetary policy best fits their project. The simplest way in token distribution is to offer the entire supply of tokens to the public, at the initial coin offering (ICO) process, so that the token supply remains a stable and predetermined number, right from the start (excluding the mining process, which further increases supply at an already known rate). In this case, there are limited tools that the token issuer can use to influence the price of the token. One of these tools is to apply a practice similar to share repurchases, known as token buybacks. Once the entire supply has been offered to the market, the token issuer can buy back a percentage of the existing tokens, therefore decreasing the circulating supply and thus increasing the price, as shown in Figure 4.2. As the chart shows, the equilibrium at a given time is at price P, where the supply (S) and the demand (D) curves intersect. If tokens are deliberately removed from the market, the circulating supply will decrease (from S to S1) and thus the price will increase (from P to P1).

There are two ways to handle the repurchased tokens. These can either be kept for future use, or they can be "destroyed", a process called "token burn". When an issuer applies the token buyback strategy regularly, this results in a regular upward trend in the token price, which satisfies long-term investors while simultaneously providing liquidity in the market since short-term investors that would like to exit can do so by selling their tokens to the issuer, who buys them back.

A second scenario, which is relatively common when tokens are issued and offered to the market, is to issue all tokens but to market some of them, for example, 70%, while the remaining 30% is held by the issuer. This way the issuer can finance operational costs but can also increase market supply in times of high demand by releasing the available tokens, while simultaneously taking advantage of the higher price and realizing their projected return.

4.3 Quantity theory of money

A token is created to serve specific purposes within a community. The fact that the token is transferrable makes it automatically a means of transferring value in the community network. In case no problems arise within the community, and its members continue to believe that they benefit from being members of the community (in other words, if the existence of the community has value),

"Tokenomics" and valuation **41**

the volume and speed of (token) transactions within the community is expected to increase. From this perspective, tokens have the characteristics of a currency, and not of an asset, and the quantitative theory of money can be used to explain token price fluctuation. The quantitative theory of money equation (equation of exchange) is the following:

$$MV = PT$$

where
 M: the total money supply (in our case is the token supply),
 V: velocity of money (tokens)
 P: the overall price level (i.e., the value of all goods and services in token terms)
 T: the total transaction volume.

The equation of exchange is an identity equation, meaning that the equation must always be true, so that MV will always have to be equal to PT. This implies that the total value of all money expenditures (MV) is equal to the total value of all items sold (PT). Also, note that (P) is the overall price *level*, which has to be distinguished from the value a single token (P_T). The value of a single token (P_T) refers to what it can buy, whereas the price level (P) refers to the average of all of the prices of goods and services in a given economy. The basic causal relationship between the price level (P) and the value of a single token (P_T) is that as the price level goes up, the value of the token goes down, so that P_T is inversely related to P: $P_T = 1/P$. The theory has two interesting implications on the price of a token P_T when viewed at the crypto market ecosystem.

First, assuming that the velocity (V) and the total transaction volume (T) are constant, an increase in token supply (M) will cause a rise in the overall price level (P). If the overall price level (P) increases, then the value of each token P_T will decrease, because as inflation rises, the purchasing power, or the value of a single token, decreases.

Second, assuming now that the token supply (M) is constant, and the velocity (V) increases, the value of a single token is also expected to decrease. That is, if a token can be used more times at a given period to buy a specific quantity of products/services, the same token is available more times to buy the same amount of goods and services. This means that the same number of tokens are recycled more often within a given time period and therefore *effective* supply is increased; this increase in the effective supply has the same consequences as the increase in token supply discussed in the previous paragraph, leading to this inverse relationship between velocity and the token value. The velocity issue is of high importance in the crypto market ecosystem, since the technology does allow higher levels of velocity when compared with the fiat currency payment infrastructure, due to faster transaction times, lower transaction costs, relatively highly liquid markets, and a global scale. On the other hand, a token that is not traded because holders are still waiting for the "true" function to be developed by the team, will tend to see higher prices, since the velocity of this particular token is low.

42 "Tokenomics" and valuation

The application of the quantity theory of money to the crypto market eco-system does not come without criticism. First, the theory best fits tokens that mainly serve as currencies and does not cover all coins in the market. Second, all factors in the money equation (M, V, P, T) cannot be easily measured or esti-mated in the crypto market ecosystem; note that in traditional economics these factors are estimated using respectively built mathematical models. Furthermore, it is hard to measure the implications a change of one variable will have to the other variables since the relationships between the variables is dynamic, so that it is problematic to assume a steady relationship among them. Note for example that, for most of the existing coins, M is constantly changing (i.e., via mining or burning), adding another layer of complexity to the estimations.

4.4 Token economics of utility

This approach refers to the utility aspect of the token. Tokens can be linked with certain rewards or benefits for their holders. A simple example is to provide dis-counts for specific products of services via using the token. This would provide incentives for consumers to buy the token to take advantage of the discounts, therefore increasing the token demand and thus the price. This process will con-tinue until the combined token price and discount it offers is still cheaper than using the fiat currency to buy the product/service. However, the focus here is the fact that the price of the token can be enhanced by linking their use with specific rewards and/or benefits.

There are interesting side effects of the utility aspect of the tokens. When tokens are linked with benefits, consumers will first have to buy them, to be able to take advantage of the reward, as already discussed above. Just after they buy them, they are expected to use either all of them or a part of them to take advantage of the inherent reward. By using them, they actually sell them usually back to the issuer, who is usually in charge of the discounted product/service, so that the issuer collects large amounts of the token that can then use them in the context of the monetary policy discussed in the previous section.

4.5 Combining the monetary policies and the economics of utility

The monetary policies and the economics of utility can be interlinked as strate-gies that affect token prices. This section discusses this combination of the factors that affect the two strategies in price determination.

Suppose that the current price equilibrium for token X is at P1 levels, where "Demand X" meets "Supply X" (Figure 4.3). The team behind the project, who also manages the token, announces a price discount of a service they offer to any token holder, while at the same time, they also decide to increase the token supply by selling part of their undistributed tokens held in the ICO. The first action (reward an-nouncement) will increase the demand of the token so that the demand curve moves to the right at "Demand 2X". The second action (increase in the token supply) moves

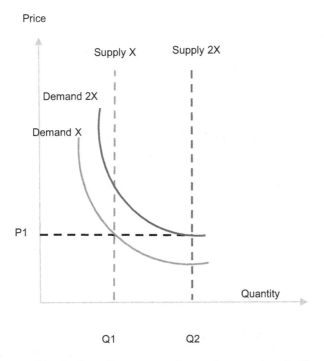

FIGURE 4.3 Combined effect of monetary policy and economics of utility.

the supply curve to the right at "Supply 2X". These two events offset each other, so that the token price level remains unchanged at the P1 level.

4.6 The discounted cash flow model

The discounted cash flow (DCF) model is a valuation model in which the value of an item (financial asset or company) is derived based on a set of assumptions about the fundamentals of a business for a prespecified future time horizon. The logic of the model is that the value of the item in question is equal to the sum of the present values of a set of future cash flows derived by the item, as follows:

$$Value = \sum_{t=1}^{n} \frac{CF_t}{(1+r)^t}$$

where
CF_t = the annual cash flow,
r = the required return
t = the number of years (1, 2, ..., n).

Assessing the DCF model in the crypto market world, the first observation is that tokens do not create cash flows, making it impossible to use. Specifically, the vast

44 "Tokenomics" and valuation

majority of tokens are not (at least yet) designed to generate recurring profits or cash flows based on a function they perform. At best, some tokens may be able to generate cash flows sometime in the future when the project they give access to develops a product or service that can be used only via the token utility rights. Some other tokens, however, are not linked with any specific project and are mainly used as currencies, so that the DCF model cannot be applied at all.

A second observation refers to the very mechanics of the models used in the context of the DCF, which involve concepts that cannot be easily applied in the crypto market. Cryptocurrencies have no exposure to most common stock market and macroeconomic factors, or to the returns of currencies and commodities, but seem to be affected only by factors inherent to the crypto market ecosystem itself, such as momentum factors and investors' attention. This implies that one should be careful when applying traditional valuation models in the crypto market world. For example, (r) in the DCF is usually the weighted average cost of capital (WACC) that includes the cost of equity, which in turn is calculated using the capital asset pricing model (CAPM). But the use of these models assumes that there are (theoretical and empirical) links between the elements that are being used (i.e., the risk-free rate and the beta coefficient) and the asset to be evaluated (i.e., the cryptocurrency), an assumption that is still questioned.

The two observations discussed above show that, to date, it is practically impossible to apply the DCF model as a commonly accepted valuation model for all cryptocurrencies.

4.7 Technical analysis

Technical analysis is perhaps the only type of traditional analysis that can be directly performed in the crypto market, exactly as performed in the traditional financial markets. It is developed within the behavioral finance context, which approaches finance and financial decision-making from a broader social science perspective including psychology and sociology. Market psychology is perceived as a decisive factor in asset price determination, so that the prediction of mass psychology can potentially lead to excess returns for investors. Technical analysis incorporates psychology into the rational approach of price determination in markets and seeks to predict future prices based on past price patterns. It is essentially a reflection of the idea that prices are driven by trends determined by the changing attitudes of investors toward a variety of economic, monetary, political, and psychological forces. It uses market data, such as past market prices and transaction volumes, to construct visual observations of market graphs and to apply specific statistical techniques, to predict future price fluctuation. This type of data is readily and freely available for anyone to use in the crypto market, and any information needed to perform technical analysis can be easily extracted by various internet sites that record cryptocurrencies' market prices. That is why technical analysis is perhaps the only type of traditional analysis that can be identically performed in the crypto market, at least in terms of the resources needed to apply the analysis.

4.7.1 Assumptions of technical analysis

There are certain assumptions needed so that the technical analysis can be performed:

1. The market discounts everything.

   Anything that affects the level of the market is reflected in prices: profit growth rate, political climate, quality of administration, current circumstances, psychological–emotional reasons (hope, fear, panic, insecurity, enthusiasm, etc.).

2. Historical trends tend to repeat themselves.

   Past market activity can be a valuable predictor for future price fluctuations. Technical analysts analyze past price patterns and are looking for signs in the current price fluctuations that resemble the patterns they have identified, so that they can predict future fluctuations based on the identified pattern.

3. Investors behavior is generally predictable.

   Investors tend to behave similarly across time and they do not change their investment behavior pattern. This can lead to market patterns that are easily observable and are expected to be repeated in the future when future and past circumstances are similar for investors to behave as they did in the past.

4. Price and volume trends can be presented in graphs giving a simple and brief overview of possible price changes.

   Price patterns can be graphically depicted. Technical analysts use graphs that show both primary past market data, such as price fluctuations over a certain period of time, plus the patterns identified, by using arrows and straight lines, to highlight the trend. This provides a simple overview of the trend identified and the possible future price movements, either within or outside the trend identified, that leads to a decision-making process based on the simultaneous analysis of the primary price fluctuation and the trend identified.

4.7.2 Tools of technical analysis and some crypto market examples

There are two main forms of analysis in technical analysis: diagrammatic analysis and mathematical-statistical analysis. Diagrammatic analysis uses specific tools such as line/bar charts, and geometrical patterns that can be identified via analyzing past price fluctuations. Mathematical-statistical analysis uses specific indicators and oscillators, which represent statistical formulations that incorporate parameters of the market psychology.

4.7.2.1 Line/bar charts

Line charts are graph lines that plot the closing prices of financial assets, providing investors a clear visualization of price fluctuations over a given time period. Bar charts are similar to line charts in purpose but contain more information on price fluctuations. Line charts use closing prices only, while "Open-high-low-close"

(OHLC) or candlestick bar charts show additional information of the intra-day price fluctuations, while maintaining the general trend revealed by the line chart. For example, Figure 4.4 shows the US dollar/bitcoin (USD/BTC) price fluctuation (plus volume fluctuation: bar charts at the bottom) during April to August 2019, using candlestick bars. The thicker part of the line (resembling a box) shows the intra-day difference between the opening and the closing prices of the day. The longer the candlesticks, the larger the intra-day price increase/decrease. The straight lines above/below the candlestick represent the highest/lowest prices during the day. Looking at Figure 4.4, a trader can identify distinct subperiods during the entire April to August period; there seem to be three upward periods (beginning of April to mid-May, beginning of June to end of June, and end of July to beginning of August), two periods of relatively high volatility (mid-May to beginning of June, and end of June to mid-July) and a downward trend (around mid-August). This is the basic type of information needed so that traders can then use to identify patterns or conduct sophisticated analysis on.

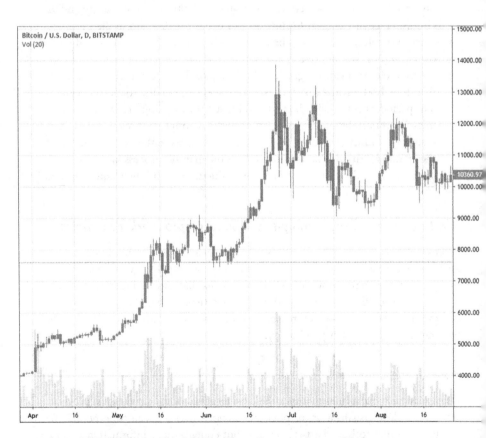

FIGURE 4.4 USD-BTC Candlestick Bar Chart: January–August 2019.

4.7.2.2 Geometrical patterns

Charting lines allow patterns to be formed. Patterns are price formations created by the price changes of a crypto-asset over time. Patterns can lead to the creation of geometrical formulations that help investors decide whether to buy or sell an asset at a specific point in time. There are several types of geometrical patterns in technical analysis, ranging from simple daily formulations to complex long-term patterns over a long period of time (several years). There are two main categories of geometrical patterns: (a) continuation patterns that show that prices are expected to follow an existing trend and (b) reversal patterns, which show that price trends are about to change, so that prices will follow an opposite direction from the existing trend.

Technical analysts try to identify these geometrical patterns to predict future prices. For example, Figure 4.5 shows BTC-USD price fluctuations from mid-May 2019 until beginning of September 2019. The black lines drawn around the fluctuating prices is an attempt to identify a pattern, in this case called the "descending triangle", to predict how prices are expected to fluctuate in the near future. This is a simple example of how traders use line/bar charts, as discussed in the previous subsection, to identify geometrical patterns to predict future price fluctuations.

4.7.2.3 Indicators and oscillators

Indicators and oscillators are technical tools that use mathematical and statistical formulations on past and current market data to help predict future price changes. Indicators create momentum signals of a crypto-asset, helping the investor identify upward or downward price trends. The main indicators and oscillators used in crypto markets are described in the paragraphs that follow.

- The moving average convergence/divergence (MACD)

The MACD is a widely used specific type of the broader category of moving averages. Moving averages, in general, reflect the underlying price trend in a way that eliminates the daily fluctuations that might disorient the investor. They demonstrate the smoothed trend of prices, providing clearer signals of buying and selling an asset according to the direction of the main trend. The term "moving" means that the average is constantly updated, via a continuous process of replacing old with new data. The MACD specifically shows the relationship of three moving averages of an asset's price and determines the momentum of an asset. This indicator is calculated by subtracting the 26-period (days/hours) exponential moving average (EMA) from the 12-period EMA and then compared to an 9-period EMA. The 12-period EMA minus 26-period EMA is called the MACD line and the 9-period EMA is called the signal line. When these lines intersect, this provides signals to investors to buy or sell. For example, Figure 4.6 is the exact same with Figure 4.4, but it also shows the MACD analysis at the bottom of the chart. The light grey line is the MACD line (12-day EMA − 26-day EMA), the dark grey line is the signal line (9-day EMA), and the tiny bars in the horizontal line show the difference

48 "Tokenomics" and valuation

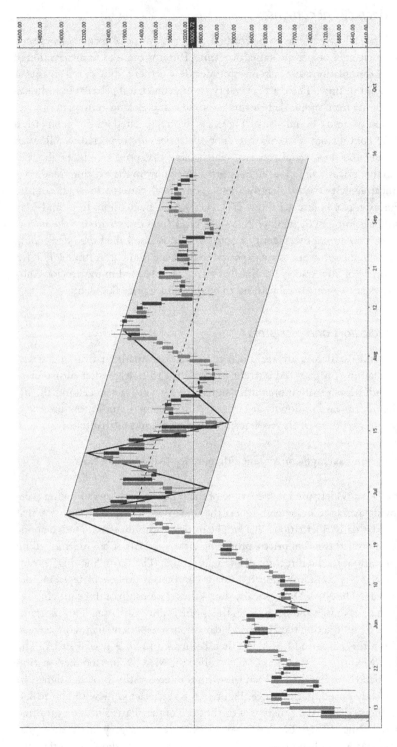

FIGURE 4.5 USD–BTC descending triangle pattern example.

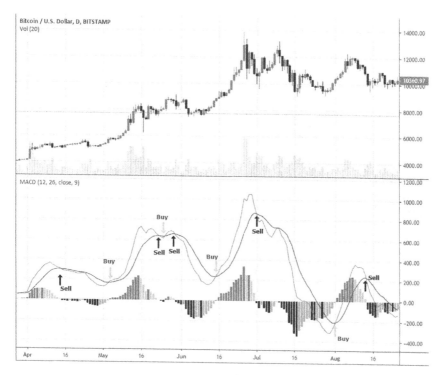

FIGURE 4.6 Example of MACD.

between the MACD and the signal lines. When the MACD line crosses from over to under the signal line, this is a sign to sell, while when the MACD line crosses from under to over the signal line, this is a sign to buy, as also shown in the chart.

- The percentage price oscillator (PPO)

The PPO is also a momentum indicator, very similar to MACD. The PPO shows the relationship between the two 26-period and 12-period EMAs (as in MACD), except the PPO measures percentage difference between the two EMAs, while the MACD measures absolute difference; specifically, the PPO is calculated as: (12-period EMA − 26-period EMA) / 26-period EMA. The PPO generates trade signals in the same way the MACD does. Figure 4.7 provides a PPO example, on the exact same price fluctuation period shown in Figure 4.4. The PPO line is the dark grey line and the signal line is the light grey line. When the PPO line crosses above the 9-period signal line from below, this is a buy signal and when the PPO line crosses below the signal line this is a sell signal. The fact that the PPO is based in percentages makes it preferable to some traders that wish to compare between assets with different prices.

- The relative strength index (RSI)

50 "Tokenomics" and valuation

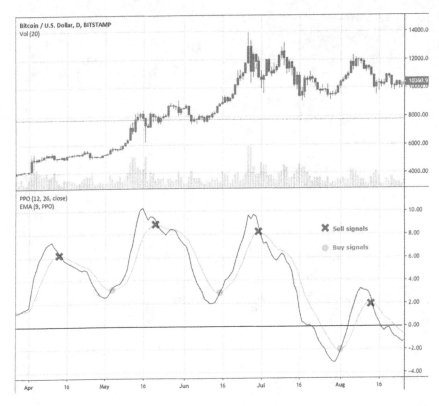

FIGURE 4.7 Example of PPO.

The RSI is another momentum indicator that measures the magnitude of price changes. It compares the magnitude of recent gains to recent losses and is used to evaluate overbought or oversold conditions in the price of an asset. It fluctuates between 0 and 100 and follows a two-step calculation process. In step 1, the relative strength (RS) over a specified period is calculated: RS = Average gains / Average losses. In step 2 the respective index is calculated as RSI = 100 − [100/(1+RS)]. Typically, if RSI readings are greater than 70, then the asset is considered to be in overbought territory, while if RSI readings are lower than 30, then the asset is considered to be in oversold territory. Readings in between are considered neutral, with the 50 level being a sign of no trend. Figure 4.8 describes how the RSI can be applied in the BTS/USD price fluctuation pattern already discussed in the previous subsections. The graph shows that the BTC is frequently overbought over the time period observed, since the RSI line crosses the 70 level 7 times during April to August 2019.

- Other types of mathematical-statistical analysis

There are several other types of mathematical-statistical analysis used in the context of technical analysis. Analysts use linear regressions to create the linear

"Tokenomics" and valuation   51

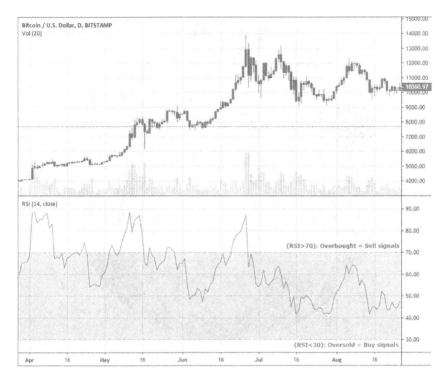

FIGURE 4.8   Example of RSI.

regression line, usually accompanied by the linear regression channel, where the latter constructs a space that leads to buy/sell indications in case the price falls below/rises above the lower/upper channel lines respectively. Based on the linear regression approach, traders also use the R-squared coefficient, which measures how closely a data set fits to the linear regression line. The closer prices move in a linear relationship with the passing of time, the stronger the trend, so that investors can evaluate the trend they are observing and whether the trend is strong or weak.

4.7.3 Technical analysis and the crypto market: exploring the EMH

The main advantage of technical analysis in the crypto market context is that all data required to perform it are already available for free and easy to get access to. Analysts have access to past and even live data on price formation and trading volumes that allow them to explore different technical analysis techniques in different time spans. The application of these techniques is not time-consuming when compared to other valuation approaches, while there is a plethora of different techniques that analysts can explore, and anyone can identify different patterns according to the sets of data employed. Furthermore, most technical analysis reports focus mainly on the most important crypto assets (bitcoin, Ethereum, ripple, etc.), leaving a big gap for the remaining altcoins to be explored.

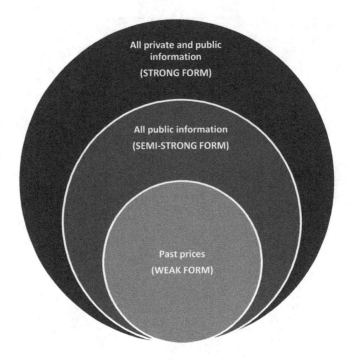

FIGURE 4.9 Different forms of efficient market hypothesis.

In this context, technical analysis seems to be the best type of traditional analysis to use in the crypto market. The question is whether technical analysis works, namely whether it yields extraordinary returns for analysts. To answer this question, one needs to explore the efficient market hypothesis (EMH). According to the EMH, asset prices reflect information, so that it is impossible to "beat the market" consistently on a risk-adjusted basis, since asset prices should only react to new information. There are three forms of pricing efficiency in the EMH (see Figure 4.9), where each one represents a different type of information that should be reflected to the asset prices, if the market is efficient.

For example, for a market to be efficient at the weak level, asset prices should already reflect all information contained in the past and current market data. For a market to be efficient at the semi-strong level, asset prices should already reflect all publicly available information, either contained in market data or in any other information source that is publicly available (i.e., financial statements, industry reports, etc.). Last, a market is efficient at the strong level when asset prices already reflect all information, either public or private.

The implication of EMH is that if the market is efficient at any level, market participants cannot consistently beat the market by making use of the respective set of information. So, if the crypto market is efficient at the weak level, analysts cannot use market data, namely technical analysis, to consistently beat the market.

"Tokenomics" and valuation **53**

Research is still in its infancy regarding the results of applying technical analysis in the crypto market. Latif et al. (2017) applied a series of different analyses to bitcoin and Litecoin to explore whether the market for these two cryptocurrencies is efficient. They concluded that the market is not efficient at the weak level, attributing their results on the fact that cryptocurrencies have no intrinsic values and prices depend on speculation. Caporale et al. (2018) reached similar conclusions finding positive correlation between past and future values for the four main cryptocurrencies (bitcoin, Litecoin, ripple, and dash) during 2013–2017, concluding that "trend trading strategies can be used to generate abnormal profits in the cryptocurrency market", a clear sign of inefficiency at the weak level. Last, Kristoufek and Vorvsda (2019) provide some mixed results. They study six main cryptocurrencies (bitcoin, dash, Litecoin, monero, ripple, and stellar) and find that they are all inefficient over the analyzed period, with the exception of July 2017 to June 2018, where most of the coins and tokens were found to be efficient. They also report different levels of efficiency, with dash being the most efficient and Ethereum and Litecoin being the least efficient.

The main conclusion is that crypto markets do not seem to be efficient at the weak level. Crypto markets are relatively new markets, with highly volatile assets, with no fundamentals, whose price fluctuation is mainly driven by speculation. In this context, technical analysis may prove beneficial for analysts, especially for those that have already been long enough in this new market, to be able to take advantage from the relatively inexperienced investors that enter the market, attracted by the potential high levels of returns achieved in the past.

Note

1 The term "token" will be used in the chapter, since it carries a broader nature and thus avoiding the limits that the terms "currencies" and "tokens" bear.

Bibliography

Andreas Hanl. (2018). "Some Insights into the Development of Cryptocurrencies." MAGKS Papers on Economics 201804, Philipps-Universitat Marburg, Faculty of Business Administration and Economics, Department of Economics. Available at: http://www.uni-marburg.de/fb02/makro/forschung/magkspapers/paper_2018/04-2018_hanl.pdf

Ashley Lannquist. (2018). "Today's Crypto Asset Valuation Frameworks, Blockchain at Berkeley." *UC Berkeley*. Available at: https://blockchainatberkeley.blog/todays-crypto-asset-valuation-frameworks-573a38eda27e

Aziz Zainuddin. (2018). "Guide to Valuing Cryptocurrency: How to Value a Cryptocurrency", *banklesstimes.com*. Available at: www.banklesstimes. com/2018/01/21/column-value-cryptocurrency/

Buterin Vitalik, Teutsch, Jason, and Christopher, Brown. (2017). "Interactive Coin Offerings." Available at: https://people.cs.uchicago.edu/~teutsch/papers/ico.pdf

Buterin Vitalik. (2017). "On Medium-of-Exchange Token Valuations."Available at: https://vitalik.ca/general/2017/10/17/moe.html

Caporale, Guglielmo Maria, Gil-Alana, Luis A., and Plastun, Oleksiy, Persistence in the Cryptocurrency Market (December 2018). DIW Berlin Discussion Paper No. 1703. Available at SSRN: https://ssrn.com/abstract=3084023 or doi:10.2139/ssrn.3084023.

Conley, J. (2017). "Blockchain and the Economics of Crypto-Tokens and Initial Coin Offerings", Vanderbilt University Department of Economics Working Papers 17-00008, Vanderbilt University Department of Economics.

Geist, Richard and Lifson Lawrence. (1999). *The Psychology of Investing*. John Wiley and Sons, New York.

Hegadekatti, Kartik. (2017). Brand Tokenization and Monetization through Cryptocurrencies. *SSRN Electronic Journal*. Available at: SSRN: https://ssrn.com/abstract=3055362 or doi:10.2139/ssrn.3055362.

Jakub, Bartos. (2015). Does Bitcoin follow the Hypothesis of Efficient Market?. *International Journal of Economic Sciences*, Vol. IV, No. 2, pp. 10–23. doi:10.20472/ES.2015.4.2.002.

Jed Grant. (2017). On Crypto Valuation – The ICO 2.0 Framework, Peer Mountain. Available at: www.peermountain.com/6P-OnCryptoValuation.pdf

Kaal, W., and Dell'Erba, M. (2017). "Initial Coin Offerings: Emerging Practices, Risk Factors, and Red Flags Forthcoming, *Fintech Handbook*, Florian Möslein and Sebastian Omlor eds., Verlag C.H. Beck (2018); U of St. Thomas (Minnesota) Legal Studies Research Paper No. 17–18." Available at: SSRN: https://ssrn.com/abstract=3067615 or doi:10.2139/ssrn.3067615.

Kaletsky, Sasha. (2018). "A Macro Framework for Valuing Crypto – All about Velocity, The Harbus, Harvard Business School." Available at: www.harbus.org/2018/macro-framework-valuing-crypto-velocity/

Kim Seoyoung, Sarin, Atulya, and Virdi, Daljeet (2018). Crypto-Assets Unencrypted. *Journal of Investment Management*. Available at: SSRN: https://ssrn.com/abstract=3117859

Kristoufek, L., and Vosvrda, M. (2019). Cryptocurrencies Market Efficiency Ranking: Not So Straightforward. *Physica A: Statistical Mechanics and Its Applications*, Vol. 531, doi:10.1016/j.physa.2019.04.089.

Latif, S. R., Mohd, M. A., Mohd Amin, M. N., and Mohamad, A. I. (2017). "Testing the weak Form of Efficient Market in Cryptocurrency." *Journal of Engineering and Applied Sciences*, Vol. 12, No. 9, pp. 2285–2288. doi:10.3923/jeasci.2017.2285.2288.

Lee David Kuo, Chuen. (2017). Invited Editorial Comment: FinTech and Alternative Investment. *The Journal of Alternative Investments Winter 2018*, Vol. 20, No. 3, pp. 6–15; Pangean Media Ltd. doi:10.3905/jai.2018.20.3.006.

Max, Hillebrand. (2017). An Introduction to Initial Coin Offerings in Project Finance, 1st Paper Version 1.0, Baden-Wuerttemberg Cooperative State University Villingen Schwenningen, Faculty of Economics.

Sehra, A., Smith, P., and Gomes, P. (2017). "Economics of Initial Coin Offerings." *Allen&Overy*. Available at: www.allenovery.com/en-gb/global/news-and-insights/publications/economics-of-initial-coin-offerings

Sid, Kalla. (2017). "A Framework for Valuing Crypto Tokens" (March 3). *CoinDesk*, Available at: www.coindesk.com/framework-valuing-crypto-tokens/

Wang, S., and Vergne, J.-P. (2017). Buzz Factor or Innovation Potential: What Explains Cryptocurrencies' Returns? *PLoS ONE*, Vol. 12, No. 1, e0169556. doi:10.1371/journal.pone.0169556

5

FUNDRAISING

Initial coin offerings

5.1 Defining initial coin offerings

Initial coin offerings (ICOs) are an innovative way to raise capital based on the blockchain technology. ICOs take place usually at an early stage of the project, and their goal is to raise funds that will cover operating costs from the start of a project to its implementation. The company that performs an ICO creates tokens (digital chips) that are then sold directly to the public. The newly issued tokens cannot be bought directly with fiat currencies (i.e., pounds, euros, etc.), and those interested in buying tokens use the main cryptocurrencies (i.e., Bitcoin, Ethereum). So, if Bob wants to buy 100 newly issued ABCD tokens, he first needs to buy the respective value of bitcoins and exchange his bitcoins with ABCD tokens.

ICOs allow fundraisers to raise capital directly from the public, at a global scale, with no transaction costs, and following a relatively easy process. These ICO features have resulted in tremendously fast and high-valued fundraising, where millions of dollars can be raised in a few hours' time. An ICO involves three parties (Figure 5.1): (i) business startups/projects that use the blockchain technology, (ii) prospective investors, and (iii) ICOs providers, which are centralized platforms on which the ICOs take place. Comparing this process with the respective IPO process in primary capital markets, both ends (projects and investors) are the same, and the substantial difference is that the fundraising facilitator is not an investment bank but an online platform, which makes use of the blockchain technology to complete the fundraising process.

To date (August 2019), the most successful ICO platform is the decentralized Ethereum network. This network offers the use of "smart contracts" where project developers can create certain computer protocols that perform, enforce, and verify the execution of the terms of a contract.

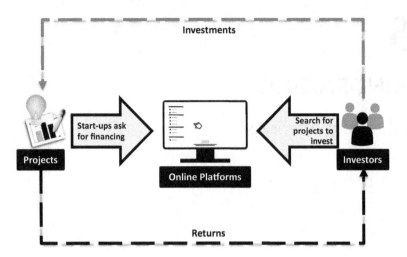

FIGURE 5.1 Main participants in an ICO.

Investors are mainly attracted by the expectation of the future success of the project. When investing, they mostly aim at capital gains, expecting that the token price will increase. Bearing in mind that the only access to the service/product that the project creates is via holding the project's tokens, and that the token supply is usually a predetermined number, if the project is successful, the token demand is expected to increase and thus the token price will also increase.

5.2 The road to ICOs

The blockchain technology was introduced in parallel with the creation of the bitcoin network in 2008. This technology was later adopted to create new altcoins. Gradually, an entire cryptocurrency ecosystem started to emerge, and five years later, the first ICO took place. In 2013, Mastercoin managed to raise 5,000 bitcoin, at a total value of $500,000. The amount raised may seem trivial when compared to the values raised in the years to come, but the successful experiment of Mastercoin, as the first ICO to be successfully implemented, was a significant milestone in this field.

It took another couple of years before ICOs started to attract considerable attention as a fundraising practice. The real explosion of ICOs came during 2016–2017, where ICOs overtook venture capital (VC) in terms of value raised (Figure 5.2), resulting in double the value raised for October–November 2017 ($3.78 billion for ICOs vs $1.88 billion for VC).

The main driver behind this rapid development of the ICO phenomenon was the combination of the following two factors: (a) the relatively very large amounts of capital raised and (b) the short time needed for the whole process to be implemented. Typical examples are FirstBlood's ICO in May 2016 that raised $5.5 million in two minutes, and the Bancor Foundation that raised $153 million

Fundraising: initial coin offerings 57

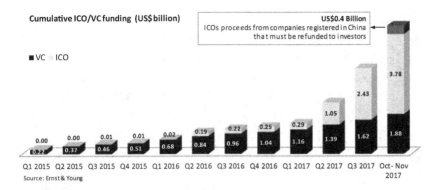

FIGURE 5.2 ICO vs. VC funding: 2015–2017.

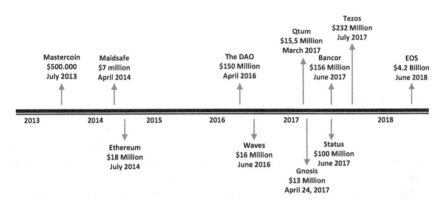

FIGURE 5.3 Ten most important ICOs during 2013–2018.

in three hours a month later. In April 2016, Gnosis project raised about $12.5 million in 12 minutes, while "Brave" startup raised $35.5 million in 30 seconds in May 2017. Figure 5.3 shows the ten most important ICOs during 2013–2017.

Regulatory authorities that were carefully monitoring the ICO trends until then decided to take action in regulating the industry, introducing stricter rules and making ICOs more difficult to implement. This change in the attitude of regulatory authorities, together with the sharp decline in the crypto market prices that followed in the beginning of 2018, have significantly contributed to the gradual fall of the volume of ICOs since then. Figure 5.4 shows the number of ICOs and the total funds raised for 2017 and 2018.

As the graph shows, there is a growing trend in total funds raised until March 2018, followed by a steady decline, which becomes sharp after July 2018. Note that the June 2017 spike is due to the completion of the year-long EOS ICO, which raised almost $4.2 billion and is, until now (August 2019), the largest ICO ever conducted. As regards the number of ICOs, this continued to increase until

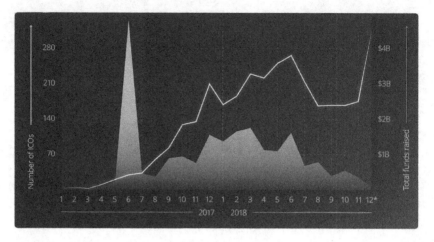

FIGURE 5.4 Number of ICOs and total funds raised: 2017 and 2018.

June 2018 and was at relatively higher levels when compared to 2017, implying that the average volume raised per ICO for 2018 was lower than that of 2017.

5.3 How ICOs work

Given that ICOs are a relatively recent phenomenon, one can observe significant case-by-case variations on how they are conducted, and there is no single process that is universally followed. However, there are specific steps that most of the ICOs seem to follow (Figure 5.5).

The first step is the pre-announcement step, which aims to inform the general public about the project. This is mainly done via announcements on forums and websites related to the blockchain technology and the crypto market (Reddit, Twitter, and Telegram). The pre-announcement provides a brief overview of the project (idea, purpose, implementation steps) and contains information about the team members behind the project. Based on these first pieces of information, the public starts providing feedback to the team. This is a very important process at these initial steps, first because it shows how the public reacts to the idea and the project itself, and second because these comments help the team refine their project until the next step, which is the offer. The offer is the final version of the project, which is officially presented and offered to the public. A central component of the offer is the white paper. The white paper is like a memorandum of understanding of the project, which contains the entire project in detail. A common structure of the white paper includes an executive summary of the project, the motivation, the main idea, and information on the marketability of the project, investor information such as token distribution schemes, information about the team and the advisors, and a roadmap of implementation. Another important part of the offer step is to present all technical features of the project, releasing the computational code of the designed application, so that experts can check any errors or gaps in the code.

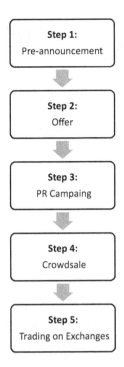

FIGURE 5.5 Main steps in an ICO.

Once the offer is made public, the team focuses on their PR campaign. Since ICOs target the general public, information dissemination plays a vital role during the whole ICO process. In fact, public relations and campaign strategies are both key factors to ICO success. Even from the first step of the pre-announcement, project owners need to make sure that they use social media channels as efficiently as possible to monitor and control information flows to the public and make use of the feedback they receive. But especially after the offer is made public, the PR campaign takes a central role in the ICO process. Project owners usually hire communication experts that advertise the forthcoming ICO, delivering speeches in conferences and online presentations, to attract investors. Part of the campaign is to use certain marketing strategies, one of the most popular of which is the so-called AirDrops. AirDrops are essentially free tokens that are distributed by project developers to the electronic wallets of the public.

The next step is the crowd sale. There are to date two different approaches on how the crowd sale is conducted. In the first case (Figure 5.6), project owners release the tokens on a specific date in the market and investors can buy them by exchanging their main cryptocurrencies (i.e., bitcoin, Ethereum) with the respective number of tokens based on the relative price of the token to the main cryptocurrency. In the second case (Figure 5.7), project owners are first funded by investors who receive their tokens later once the project has already been developed at a certain stage.

60 Fundraising: initial coin offerings

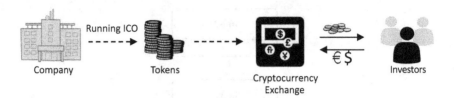

FIGURE 5.6 Fundraising in parallel with token release.

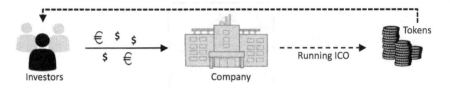

FIGURE 5.7 Fundraising prior to token release.

The crowd sale is a sensitive step in the whole process, since this is the core step in fundraising. To increase trust and transparency, several ICO issuers use escrow services and even escrow-based milestones. Escrow is a financial arrangement that involves a third party who is in charge of payments and transactions and who regulates disbursement of the funds. These third parties collect and store the capital raised from the investors in an escrow account and then disburse these funds to the issuer once a set of pre-agreed conditions, known to investors, is fulfilled. This process increases the level of trust between the project team and the funders, and thus increases the possibility of success of the ICO. Escrow-based milestones mean that the project team does not gain access to the entire capital raised at once, but these funds are released in parts and according to specific milestones that the issuers have self-set. This process further increases trust since investors view escrow-based milestones as a way to increase productivity and fulfil the goals described in the white paper because the project team can only get access to the funds raised only when these milestones are reached.

The last step is to list the newly issued coin to an exchange. There are more than 200 cryptocurrency exchanges to date with ranging listing fees and requirements. Listing a new coin to an exchange requires filling in a lengthy listing form, with information about the project and the team, as well as technical details about the coin/token. Top exchanges require legal form (i.e., the issuer must be a legal entity) plus a legal opinion letter written by a law firm, which describes the legal features of the coin, mainly focusing on whether the coin is regulated by an authority and whether any licensing applies. Some exchanges also ask for a smart contract security audit, which can take up to a month. Once the application and all the required paperwork is ready, it takes a couple of weeks until the exchange checks the application and lists the token.

5.4 Main features of an ICO

Although ICOs is a quite recent and constantly evolving phenomenon, the way ICOs are conducted already shows how it has clear differentiation from other fundraising types. In general, ICOs are quick, global, easy to participate in, broad in scope regarding what they finance, not directly regulated, focus on very early stages of project development, and are highly risky for investors. These features are further discussed in the paragraphs that follow.

There is no direct regulatory framework on how ICOs should be conducted. As a result, there are to date either very loose or no specific regulatory restrictions for both investors and fundraisers. Given that ICOs can be conducted at a global scale, this lack of a specific regulatory framework can lead to certain risks for investors that are to date highlighted by most of the main regulatory authorities worldwide.

Most ICOs take place even before the existence of the services or goods they are supposed to fund, which further increases the risks undertaken by the investors. Another feature of ICOs is that they are not financed directly by fiat currencies, and investors must use certain cryptocurrencies to buy tokens. Furthermore, most ICOs last for a very short period of time, which means that fundraising takes place very quickly.

Last, ICOs are based exclusively on the blockchain technology, meaning that they are run on decentralized electronic platforms. Funds are transferred directly to fundraisers, thereby eliminating the need for intermediaries, which significantly reduces fundraising costs. This direct financing means that fundraisers can make use of the funds raised much more quickly than in conventional fundraising practices. Also, the fact that fundraisers receive the main cryptocurrencies exchanging their newly issued tokens is another positive feature for them since these specific cryptocurrencies can be directly converted to fiat currencies. A positive feature for investors is that there are digital trading platforms on which they can exchange their tokens and can thus liquidate their investment relatively easily without any early redemption penalty. The existence of this secondary market is a very important feature for investors since there is usually no secondary market in the conventional venture capital investments, where the liquidation time horizon for investors in start-ups usually lasts for years.

5.5 Tokens

Tokens are the main transaction vehicles that ICOs use. We briefly introduced tokens in Chapter 3 and this section will now focus on the features of tokens from an ICO perspective. In Chapter 3 we saw that tokens and cryptocurrencies share some common features, but they also differ in the range of functions they perform. They are both decentralized convertible virtual tools that use cryptography to operate in a distributed, decentralized, and secure environment. They are both viewed as the digital representation of a value that can be digitally transferred and they can function as a medium of exchange, a store of value, and a unit of account. But tokens perform a broader role and are not restricted to being just a "currency", providing to their holders privileged access to the product or service for which they are issued. The term *cryptocurrencies* puts emphasis on transactions, while the term *tokens* emphasizes (the broader) utility.

There are fundamental differences between ICO tokens and IPO shares. Tokens differ from shares in their purpose and nature. They do not carry ownership rights but provide utility rights and are more project-oriented than shares, which are more cash flow–oriented. This project-oriented nature provides a form of uniqueness to each and every token. Since project A is different from project B, the tokens that will be issued and sold to finance these two projects, respectively, will also provide access to different functions. This uniqueness of each token is made possible via the use of smart contracts.

Each token has value only within the system it operates. It is an integral part of the project it was designed to finance. In this sense, the token has a dual purpose: (a) to raise funds for the project owner and (b) to provide access to the product itself for the holder. Each token incorporates minimum obligations of the issuer (project owner) to the holder and the real value of the token depends on the utility they have in the operating network they function within. This utility can exist in different forms, depending on each project itself, and, to date, there is no formal categorization of different groups of utilities.

5.6 The importance of white paper in ICOs

The first whitepaper was the bitcoin white paper, issued in 2008. Since then, almost all projects use white papers to explain the project to the public. Particularly in recent years, where the crypto market has gradually moved closer to being a form of investment, white papers started to play a central role in the ICO process.

White papers must be explanatory, understandable, and clear. They are the most important information vehicle between the project team and the funders/investors, and they are similar in purpose with the prospectus in IPOs. So far, and contrary to the IPO prospectus, there are no official regulatory requirements that an ICO white paper will have comply with. Each team decides on what information to disclose, but the majority of white papers tend to include the following information: (a) the idea of the project, what it aims to achieve, prospects, and risks involved; (b) investor information, such as token creation and distribution, token usage and rights, geographical coverage (some countries might be excluded due to regulatory obstacles); (c) a clear timetable per implementation stage; and (d) information about the team behind the project.

The problem-idea issue needs to be described very clearly, and an extensive reference to the service that the project will create needs to be made, so that funders can understand the purpose of the project. The team of the project needs to demonstrate that they understand the goals and motives of potential investors

Fundraising: initial coin offerings **63**

and any technical risks that may arise while implementing the project should be clearly discussed.

Clear information should also be disclosed on the process of token creation and distribution, such as the total number of tokens to be issued, the percentage of tokens that remain to the team and/or the advisers, the way the tokens will be created and distributed in the future, etc. The white paper will also need to refer to the type of rights that the tokens offer to their holders and how the tokens can be used in the context of the project.

The white paper must also provide a clear timetable spread over the various implementation stages. Most projects include several implementation stages/milestones and the project team will need to show information on when they expect to reach them and how they will be financed. In most cases, these milestones are also linked with funding release from the capital raised at the ICO stage, as already discussed previously.

Information on team members is of vital importance as well, even though the ICO practice did not start with providing enough information about the team. The first ICOs did not refer extensively to team members, but as ICOs attracted investors' interest, this gradually changed. In fact, bearing in mind that most projects are at seed level, the team behind each project is one of the most important information that investors should be looking at. The white paper will need to make extensive reference to each member of the team, to their experience, skills, talent, and how they are linked with the project.

White papers are this one key document where all ICO details come together and are synthesized. It must provide a prospective investor/funder a full picture of the project and give them enough information to make an informed decision. This document should aim at building confidence to funders/investors about the idea of the project, about the reality of its implementation, and about the capability of the team to bring it through.

5.7 Comparing ICOs with IPOs and crowdfunding

The closest traditional fundraising types that ICOs can be compared with, are initial public offerings (IPOs) and crowdfunding. ICOs share some common features with IPOs and crowdfunding, but they also have significant differences, as discussed in the following subsections.

5.7.1 ICOs and IPOs

The main objective for both ICOs and IPOs is to raise capital. Both ends are the same, meaning that project owners/entrepreneurs are looking to raise funds from funders/investors. However, there are some very significant differences between the two.

In IPOs, investors become shareholders in established companies that already have developed their own company assets and have long started generating cash flows. Investors receive shares, which represent ownership of the company, at a certain percentage based on the number of shares they buy. As shareholders, investors in an IPO have voting rights on significant company decisions, and they are entitled to receive compensation in case the company is bankrupt and liquidated. Last, the means of return for IPO investors are usually two: dividends and capital gains. On the other hand, ICOs take place at a very early growth stage of a project, usually at seed stages of a startup, that has no ready product or service, and thus no cash flows yet. Investors receive digital tokens that give them access to and privileged usage of a future product or service. Token holders do not have (at the majority of ICOs to date) any ownership rights on the company that runs the project and thus no dividend or compensation rights in case of liquidation. They mainly aim at capital gains, expecting that the demand of the token will increase once the product/service is created, so that the price of the token will also increase, given that the token supply is a predetermined number of tokens.

Pricing also differs significantly. In IPOs, there are certain valuation practices applied to price the newly issued shares, and the IPO company usually hires investment banks that help them determine a fair price based on a list of factors linked with the company and the market. In ICOs, pricing is a very difficult task since no fundamental analysis can be applied, first, because of the absence of track record data, and, second, because of the very nature of the ICO, which is difficult to monetize. In terms of price fluctuation, there are no market rules in the crypto market (i.e., market limits, order size limitations) to prevent extreme volatility and large token holders are more able to manipulate the market since there are no lock-up periods for founders/entrepreneurs.

Another important difference is the level of intermediation. Most IPOs are handled by underwriters who are heavily involved with many aspects of the IPO, from providing advice and filing documents to undertaking the entire offering. In the case of ICOs, project owners are more heavily involved, and the role of advisers is significant, but not at such high levels as in the IPOs. Last, IPOs are heavily regulated and there are specific requirements around offerings, marketing, and disclosure. In the case of ICOs, regulatory requirements are either unclear or inexistent. Table 5.1 summarizes the main differences between ICOs and IPOs, as discussed in the paragraphs above.

5.7.2 ICOs: crowdfunding

ICOs are often referred to as blockchain crowdfunding. These two funding forms are closer to one another than ICOs and IPOs, for the following four main reasons: (a) they both take place at an early growth stage of the company/project, (b) they both make use of online technology infrastructure more than in the case of IPOs, (c) they both make extensive use of social media for disseminating information, and (d) retail investors take a more central part at their campaign in both forms when compared with IPOs that aim relatively more at institutional

Fundraising: initial coin offerings **65**

TABLE 5.1 ICOs vs. IPOs

	IPOs	ICOs
Issuers	Established companies	Startups
Investors	Institutional and private/ mutual funds	Everyone/blockchain supporters globally
Investors receive	Shares	Tokens
Return of investment	Dividends/capital gains	Access to/privilege usage of a future product/service
Duration of offerings	Lengthy	Short
Access to offerings	Limited availability	Open to anyone
Pricing	Certain valuation methods	Challenging valuation
Track record data	Balance sheets	No track records
Intermediation	Investment banks/ underwriters	Project owners/advisors
Regulation	Regulated by financial authorities	Not currently regulated

investors. However, there are still significant differences between the two, as discussed in the following paragraphs.

First, there are already clear categories in crowdfunding that are widely recognized in official regulatory documents. Specifically, a widely followed categorization, based on the type of reward that the funder receives, is the following: (a) donation, (b) reward, (c) lending - peer-to-peer, minibonds, and (d) equity crowdfunding. This allows the development of specific regulatory requirements per type and to date the regulatory requirements for crowdfunding with financial returns (points c and d) are stricter than those of donation- and rewards-based crowdfunding. In the case of ICOs, there is no such clear categorization to group projects to categories with similar features. The fact that different crowdfunding forms are recognized gives rise to another main difference between the two financing forms: in all ICOs, funders receive tokens, while in crowdfunding funders may receive nothing (donation), or something nonfinancial (reward), or a financial security (equity crowdfunding) or a claim (peer-to-peer lending).

In terms of product development, products/services in the case of crowdfunding are usually at a slightly more advanced level when compared to ICOs. A very important difference between the two financing forms is that tokens are traded in a secondary market, while there is no such market in the case of crowdfunding (with a few individual exceptions that are due to platform initiatives). This means first that there is a price for tokens and second that investors have an exit option, two very important features for investors, that crowdfunding does not offer.

Last, the use of blockchain technology in ICOs results in a couple of payment-related differences as well. In crowdfunding campaigns, fundraising is done through traditional channels such as bank accounts and credit cards and project owners receive the funds raised in fiat currencies. While in ICOs, project owners

TABLE 5.2 ICOs vs crowdfunding

	ICOs	*Crowdfunding*
Regulation	Not currently regulated	Regulatory requirements per type
Investors	Everyone/blockchain supporters globally	Angel investors/early supporters
Investors receive	Tokens	Donation/reward/financial security/claims
Product development	Concept/idea	Advanced level
Secondary markets	Yes	No
Intermediation	Blockchain platform	Online crowdfunding platforms
Fundraising channels	Blockchain technology	Banks, credit cards
Funding currency	Crypto	Fiat
Risk	High	Medium

receive cryptocurrencies for selling their tokens and the payment transactions take place via the use of the blockchain technology without the need of a financial institution. Table 5.2 summarizes the main differences between ICOs and crowdfunding, as discussed in the paragraphs above.

Bibliography

Abgaryan, A., Liu, L., Menteshashvili, T., Abgaryan, S., and Gao, C. (2017). Aimwise: Decentralized ICO Servicing Platform, White Paper (July 20).

Adhami, Saman, Giudici, Giancarlo, and Martinazzi, Stefano. (2017). Why Do Businesses Go Crypto? An Empirical Analysis of Initial Coin Offerings. *Journal of Economics and Business*, 9 May 2018. Available at: SSRN: https://doi.org/10.1016/j.jeconbus.2018.04.001Get

Belleflamme, Paul, Omrani, Nessrine, and Peitz, Martin. (2015). "The Economics of Crowdfunding Platforms." Available at: SSRN: https://ssrn.com/abstract=2585611 or doi:10.2139/ssrn.2585611.

Bennouri, Moez, and Falconieri, Sonia. (2004). "The Optimal Design of IPOs: Price vs Quantity Discrimination." Available at: SSRN: https://ssrn.com/abstract=491002 or doi:10.2139/ssrn.491002.

Brant, Downes. (2017). "Trends in Token Sales Proposals." *Smith&Crown* (September 8). Available at: www.smithandcrown.com/trends-token-sale-proposals/

Cerezo Sánchez, David. (2017). "An Optimal ICO Mechanism." Available at: SSRN: https://ssrn.com/abstract=3040343 or doi:10.2139/ssrn.3040343.

Chang, Jen-Wen. (2016). "The Economics of Crowdfunding" (August 30). Available at: SSRN: https://ssrn.com/abstract=2827354 or doi:10.2139/ssrn.2827354.

Conley, J.P. (2017). "Blockchain and the Economics of Crypto-Tokens and Initial Coin Offerings." Vanderbilt University Department of Economics Working Papers 17-00008, Vanderbilt University Department of Economics.

Diemers, Daniel. (2017). "Initial Coin Offerings and a Strategic Perspective on ICOs, Briefing Document, Strategic & pwc." Available at: https://finance20.ch/web/wp-content/uploads/2017/09/20170913_Strategic-Implications-of-ICO_PwC-Strategy_DanielDiemers_vF.pdf

Ellman, Matthew, and Hurkens, Sjaak. (2014). "Optimal Crowdfunding Design" (October 1). NET Institute Working Paper No. 14–21. Available at: SSRN: https://ssrn.com/abstract=2507457 or doi:10.2139/ssrn.2507457.

EY Research: Initial Coin Offerings (ICOs), Ernst & Young. (2017, December). Available at:. www.ey.com/Publication/vwLUAssets/ey-research-initial-coin-offerings-icos/$File/ey-research-initial-coin-offerings-icos.pdf

EY Study: Initial Coin Offerings (ICOs), The Class of 2017 – One Year Later, Ernst & Young. (2018, October). Available at: https://assets.ey.com/content/dam/ey-sites/ey-com/en_gl/news/2018/10/ey-ico-research-web-oct-17-2018.pdf

Fenu, G., Marchesi, L., Marchesi, M., and Tonelli, R. (2018). The ICO Phenomenon and Its Relationships, with Ethereum Smart Contract Environment, *2018 International Workshop on Blockchain Oriented Software Engineering (IWBOSE)*, 26–32. doi:10.1109/IWBOSE.2018.8327568.

Flood, John, and Robb, Lachlan. (2017). Trust, Anarcho-Capitalism, Blockchain and Initial Coin Offerings. Griffith University Law School Research Paper No. 17–23; University of Westminster School of Law Research Paper. SSRN: https://ssrn.com/abstract=3074263 or doi:10.2139/ssrn.3074263.

François, Derrien, and Kent, Womack. (2003). Auctions vs. Bookbuilding and the Control of Underpricing in Hot IPO Markets. *Review of Financial Studies*, Vol. 16, No. 1, pp. 31–61. Available at: http://citeseerx.ist.psu.edu/viewdoc/download?doi=10.1.1.322.2150&rep=rep1&type=pdf

Gatto, James. (2017). "Initial Coin Offerings – An Alternative Funding Mechanism for Startups." *Sheppard Mullin Richter & Hampton LLP*. Available at: www.itechlaw.org/sites/default/files/Startup.pdf

Morgan, Joshua S. (2018). What I Learned Trading Cryptocurrencies While Studying the Law, 25U. *Miami International & Comparative Law Review*, Vol. 159, Available at: https://repository.law.miami.edu/umiclr/vol25/iss1/6

Kaal, W., and Dell'Erba, M. (2018). Initial Coin Offerings: Emerging Practices, Risk Factors, and Red Flags. In: Möslein, F., and Omlor, S. (eds) *Fintech Handbook*. Verlag Beck, München.

Kastelein, Richard. (2017). What Initial Coin Offerings Are and Why VC Firms Care, *Harvard Business Review* (24 March). Available at: https://hbr.org/2017/03/what-initialcoin-offerings-are-and-why-vc-firms-care

Kuo, Chuen, David, Lee, Guo, Li, and Wang, Yu. (2017). "Cryptocurrency: A New Investment Opportunity?" Available at: SSRN: https://ssrn.com/abstract=2994097 or doi:10.2139/ssrn.2994097.

Lawrence, Lundy, Jamie, Burke, and Aron van, Ammers. (2016). "All You Need to Know About Initial Coin Offerings: The Tension Between Business Model Innovation and Securities Regulation." Outlier Ventures Research, a Division of Outlier Ventures. Available at: https://www.the-blockchain.com/docs/Initial_Coin_Offerings_Outlier_Ventures_Research.pdf

Lee David Kuo Chuen. (2017). Invited Editorial Comment: FinTech and Alternative Investment. *The Journal of Alternative Investments Winter 2018*, Vol. 20, No. 3, pp. 6–15; Pangean Media Ltd. doi:10.3905/jai.2018.20.3.006.

Malakhov, Alexey. (2013). "The Role of Uninformed Investors in an Optimal IPO Mechanism, or What Google Did Right and Facebook Did Wrong" (August 5). Available at: SSRN: https://ssrn.com/abstract=687167 or doi:10.2139/ssrn.687167.

Massey, R., Dalal, D., and Dakshinamoorthy, A. (2017). "Initial Coin Offering: A New Paradigm." Deloitte. Available at: www2.deloitte.com/content/dam/Deloitte/us/Documents/process-andoperations/us-cons-new-paradigm.pdf

OECD. (2019). "Initial Coin Offerings (ICOs) for SME Financing." Available at: www.oecd.org/finance/initial-coin-offerings-for-sme-financing.htm

Pietrewicz, Lesław. (2017). Emerging Trends in Entrepreneurial Finance: The Rise of ICOs. doi:10.13140/RG.2.2.31498.77764.

Praveen, Kumar, Nisan, Langberg, and David, Zvilichovsky. (2015). (Crowd)funding Innovation. *SSRN Electronic Journal*. Available at: https://papers.ssrn.com/sol3/papers.cfm?abstract_id=2600923

Rohr, J., and Wright, A. (2017). Blockchain-Based Token Sales, Initial Coin Offerings, and the Democratization of Public Capital Markets. Cardozo Legal Studies Research Paper No. 527; University of Tennessee Legal Studies Research Paper No. 338. Available at: SSRN: https://ssrn.com/abstract=3048104 or doi:10.2139/ssrn.3048104.

Siegel, Dirk, Brosig, Mark, Giessen, Wanja A., Gramatke, Mirko R., Heinzelmann, Sven, Kumar, Sawan S., and Paulsen, Jens H. (2017). "ICOs – the New IPOs? How to Fund Innovation in the Crypto Age." Blockchain Institute, Deloitte. Available at: www2.deloitte.com/content/dam/Deloitte/de/Documents/Innovation/ICOs-the-new-IPOs.pdf

Smith and Crown. (2017). "Overview and Analysis of ICO Regulatory Developments." *Smith + Crown* (September 20). www.smithandcrown.com/overview-analysis-ico-regulatory-developments/

Timothy, McKenna, and Sammy, Chu. (2017). "A Look at Initial Coin Offerings." NERA Economic Consulting (December 12), p. 1. Available at: www.nera.com/content/dam/nera/publications/2017/PUB_A_ Look_at_ICOs_1217.pdf

Yadav, Mohit. (2017). "Exploring Signals for Investing in an Initial Coin Offering (ICO)" (September 1). Available at: SSRN: https://ssrn.com/abstract=3037106 or doi:10.2139/ssrn.3037106.

Yan, Chen. (2018). Blockchain Tokens and the Potential Democratization of Entrepreneurship and Innovation. *Business Horizons*. Available at: www.sciencedirect.com/science/article/pii/S0007681318300375 or doi:10.1016/j.bushor.2018.03.006.

6

THE REGULATORY FRAMEWORK

6.1 Introduction

Regulatory intervention is a critical survival factor at the early stages of any innovation. Regulation can either destroy or enhance and further develop anything new that has grown enough to attract it. The crypto market could not be an exception. Regulators were at first indifferent when bitcoin was launched and started having a closer look at the crypto market when the latter started getting larger. A key year was 2017, when the amount of funds invested in ICOs globally was more than double the amount invested via VC. This attracted the attention of regulators, who had remained silent for a long time about this phenomenon, and in 2017, the time has come to start looking deeper in this area.

Regulatory authorities of most countries are mainly concerned about ICOs because they carry high levels of risk for investors due to the lack of a clear regulatory framework. As regulators started investigating this new phenomenon that exploded in a very short period of time, they came across a difficult puzzle to solve; how tokens are defined, what their specific features are, and, in particular, how close they are to financial assets. If tokens are similar to financial assets, they could be treated as such and little adjustments need to be made in the existing regulation for financial assets and the respective markets. But, as discussed, tokens and financial assets show some significant differences that make the job of regulators a difficult puzzle to solve.

The purpose of this chapter is to explore the regulatory framework in the crypto market and particularly how the most important jurisdictions approach ICOs. The specific case of ICOs is chosen since the fundraising process attracts high levels of regulatory scrutiny in traditional markets; however, several references are made to other parts of the crypto market from a regulatory perspective as well. The information provided in this chapter was constantly updated until

70 The regulatory framework

the summer of 2019 and may be out of date by the time you read the chapter. However, the sections that follow provide at least a picture of how the main jurisdictions globally treated ICOs at the very beginning of this phenomenon, plus they provide sources that allow the reader to update their own knowledge about recent developments. The countries are listed in a calendar order, according to when they published an official document that made direct reference on how ICOs should be regulated.

6.2 United States

The US authorities became the first major jurisdiction to take a stand on how they plan to regulate ICOs. On July 25, 2017, the US Securities and Exchange Commission (SEC) published their report[1] of investigation for the decentralized autonomous organization (DAO),[2] a virtual organization embodied in computer code and executed on blockchain, asking "the threshold question whether DAO Tokens are securities" and concluding that they indeed are, according to the Federal Securities Law.

In the press release that accompanied the report,[3] the SEC said that "issuers of distributed ledger or blockchain technology-based securities must register offers and sales of such securities unless a valid exemption applies" and that "securities exchanges providing for trading in these securities must register unless they are exempt". This practically meant that ICOs must register with the SEC, must receive a special license, and must register the issued digital tokens.

In September 2017, the SEC created the Cyber Unit,[4] whose role was to look for illegal activities on cyberspace, including the distributed ledger technology (DLT).

To date (August 2019), there is no law prohibiting ICOs in the United States, the authorities use a slightly more open approach regarding whether tokens should be treated as securities, and the SEC emphasizes the following "5 things to know"[5]:

1. ICOs can be securities offerings.

    ICOs, based on specific facts, may be securities offerings, and fall under the SEC's jurisdiction of enforcing federal securities laws.
2. They may need to be registered.

    ICOs that are securities most likely need to be registered with the SEC or fall under an exemption to registration.
3. Tokens sold in ICOs can be called many things.

    ICOs, or more specifically tokens, can be called a variety of names, but merely calling a token a "utility" token or structuring it to provide some utility does not prevent the token from being a security.
4. ICOs may pose substantial risks.

    While some ICOs may be attempts at honest investment opportunities, many may be frauds. They may also present substantial risks for loss or manipulation, including through hacking, with little recourse for victims after-the-fact.

5. Ask questions before investing.

Th SEC urges potential investors to ask questions and demand clear answers before investing.

6.3 Singapore

Singapore is the first country in Asia (and third in the world) where ICOs took place.[6] Singapore has long been a worldwide destination for startups, mainly because the state provides several incentives for startups such as specific funding and tax incentives. Several promising projects have already been launched in Singapore, via the country's fintech support program in cooperation with the Monetary Authority of Singapore (MAS) and the central bank of the country. MAS supports ICOs in order to maintain the country's position, not only as an important financial center, but also as a country of innovation.

On August 10, 2017, and shortly after the SEC's press release regarding the ICOs, MAS issued a similar press release[7] stating that ICOs and the tokens that emerge respectively will be regulated by MAS, provided that they are products that fall under the Securities and Futures Act (SFA). Furthermore, they informed potential investors about the risks of ICOs, pointing out that the majority of them are uncertain investments promising high returns and with insufficient liquidity in the secondary market. They also provided advice on the measures that should be taken by those who wish to get involved in an ICO.

Three months later, in November 2017, MAS issued a "Guide to Digital Token Offerings"[8] that aimed to provide general guidance on the application of the Singaporean securities laws in relation to offers or issues of digital tokens. The content of the guide had no legal validity and it did not amend or replace any existing laws, regulations, or requirements. According to the guide, any ICO or token that has the characteristics of a capital market product (i.e., capital market securities, debt securities, futures, contracts negotiating future currency leverage, etc.) will be regulated by the MAS.

The guide also mentioned that the authorities would examine the structure and characteristics of, including the rights attached to, the issued tokens per project, to determine if the they can fall under the definition of any type of a capital markets product under the SFA. Such products are tokens that may represent: (i) ownership interest in a corporation or a business trust, (ii) a debenture, or any evidence of indebtedness, (iii) a derivatives contract, and (iv) a unit in a collective investment scheme (i.e., funds). The guide also included some case studies with examples, to clarify when the SFA applies to ICOs, noting that these case studies "are not indicative or determinant" of the way the Authority will decide whether the ICOs fall under the law, as each one will be checked on a case by case basis.

The guide was updated in April 2019,[9] and MAS added that all intermediaries in an ICO are subject to law and are required to respect the guidelines based on

Anti-Money Laundering (AML) and Countering Financing of Terrorism (CFT) policies. Intermediaries were clarified as being any party involved in an ICO process, such as token issuers, operators of ICOs platforms, trading platforms, and financial advisers. The guide also stated that the ICO platform should hold a license for the provision of capital market services as well as the financial advisers should be licensed to provide financial advice.

Finally, the latest guide included information on the implementation of a regulatory sandbox[10] for the MAS regulated tokens. In this context, any company wishing to use innovative technologies to provide financial services regulated by MAS could apply to join the regulatory sandbox scheme. MAS assumes that the interested companies take all the necessary due diligence measures before applying and that they are aware of the legal and regulatory requirements for the development of the proposed financial service. Once the application is approved, MAS would provide the appropriate regulatory support, relaxing the specific legal and regulatory requirements. These latest advancements show that Singapore aims at strengthening the regulatory framework for ICOs, rather than adopting a harsh stance against this new industry.

6.4 Canada

Cryptocurrencies are considered by law to be "commodities" since 2013 in Canada. ICOs are permitted and any trading capital gains are taxed. The Canadian Securities Administrators (CSA) published (August 24, 2017) a framework[11] to regulate ICOs and said that when the issued token has the characteristics of financial securities or derivatives, the Securities Act applies. According to the Authority, ICOs that seek to raise capital should initially check whether this capital falls under the category of financial securities and should contact the country regulators to discuss possible approaches to comply with securities laws.

On March 14, 2019, CSA and the Investment Industry Regulatory Organization of Canada (IIROC) issued a joint consultation paper[12] suggesting a regulatory framework for new trading platforms specializing in crypto-assets; this showed a clear signal that the authorities were interested in developing a clear regulatory framework for the cryptocurrency exchange platforms, aiming at providing greater integrity in cryptocurrency markets while protecting investors.

6.5 China and South Korea

China is the first country that officially banned ICOs. On September 8, 2017, a public notice signed by several institutions in China was issued, which immediately banned ICOs.[13] The notice recognized that a large number of ICOs had recently taken place, giving rise to speculation and inviting suspicion of illegal financial activities. Also, all the issuers whose ICOs had been completed were asked to return the money raised back to the investors. The measures to reduce the ICOs included prohibiting applications and platforms on websites through which ICOs are conducted and revocation of licenses to those who conducted ICOs, while banks in the country were prohibited to provide directly or indirectly such services. The public notice, however, did leave it open to lift the ban in the future, when market conditions are more mature.

In South Korea, the initial position for ICOs was to regulate them as securities' issues. However, in September 2017,[14] the Financial Stability Committee (FSC) of South Korea banned all ICOs stating that such activities hide many risks and require careful control and continuous monitoring and imposed severe penalties on those who were involved in ICOs issues. It should be noted that the ban only applied to ICOs, and cryptocurrency transactions in South Korea were still allowed, and since January 2018, all cryptocurrencies transactions are carried out with the real name of the owner to prevent money laundering.

6.6 United Kingdom

The UK is a country that is traditionally open to new technologies and therefore the UK authorities did not consider digital coins as a threat. On the contrary, the regulatory authorities expressed their encouragement on the innovative applications of startups that use the blockchain technology.

In a discussion paper that was published in April 2017,[15] the Financial Conduct Authority (FCA) stated that depending on how ICOs are structured, some of them may also fall under the existing regulatory framework. This may happen because ICOs have many common features with IPOs, therefore they might need to be approved by the FCA. The FCA also considered that tokens can be transferable securities, therefore they should fall under the respective regulatory regime.

On September 12, 2017, FCA issued a warning[16] to investors about the risks of ICOs, characterizing them as "high risk speculative investments". The risks particularly highlighted were the incomplete information that some ICOs can provide to investors, the risk of fraud, and the highly volatile prices of tokens. They also pointed out that many ICOs were based abroad and were thus not regulated by the FCA, so that in case of fraud investors are not protected by the respective agencies of Britain. At the same time, they stressed that even though companies' intentions may be in good faith, the fact that ICOs plans were at an experimental stage may put investors at risk. Therefore, they suggested, investors should carry out a thorough research, prior to an investment in an ICO, to ensure that they are confident about the quality of the project (business plan, technology, parties involved) and to be even prepared to lose the entire invested capital.

In October 2018, the Cryptoassets Task Force, in collaboration with FCA, HM Treasury, and the Bank of England, published a report[17] on the impact of crypto-assets and the DLT on financial services. The report referred to several examples of crypto-assets and other DLT applications that drove innovation in financial services, but it also mentioned specific risks that have been identified regarding consumers, market integrity, and financial crime. The report concluded that the authorities should take measures to address these risks and encourage

74 The regulatory framework

innovation in the future. Thus, in January 2019, the FCA issued a consultation paper[18] discussing guidelines on where crypto-assets interact with the current regulatory "perimeter", while they said that they could assist businesses that operate in the relevant field.

Another important part of this paper was that the FCA divided tokens into the following three distinct categories, where different rules could be applied:

Exchange tokens: These tokens currently fall outside the regulatory perimeter, and, therefore, "the transferring, buying and selling of these tokens, including the commercial operation of cryptoasset exchanges for the exchange of tokens, are activities not currently regulated by the FCA".

Security tokens: These tokens meet the definition of a Specified Investment and, possibly, a Financial Instrument under MiFID II. These tokens fall within the scope of the FCA and finance regulation.

Utility tokens: The FCA states that "as utility tokens do not typically exhibit features that would make them the same as securities, they will not be captured in the regulatory regime, unless they meet the definition of e-money".

6.7 Australia

Australia also maintains a positive attitude toward ICOs and was one of the first countries to issue regulatory guidelines for ICOs. On September 28, 2017, Australian Securities and Investment Committee (ASIC) issued a regulatory guide[19] for startups that intend to launch ICOs. In this guide, ASIC recognized the dynamics of ICOs and the fact that they contribute significantly to fundraising activities, but they pointed out that every ICO should comply with the relevant laws. They also stated that ICOs that aim to raise capital must notify the regulatory authorities, register with them, and obtain a special license. Last, companies that use ICOs must keep a record of the tokens, while in case the ICO offers derivative products, a special license is required. Finally, the Australian government introduced draft legislation for an enhanced regulators sandbox,[20] allowing fintech startups to operate under a special regulatory environment, to enable new and innovative financial technology products and services to be tested.

6.8 Switzerland

Switzerland is already known for its progressive banking regulations, and it also proves to be one of the friendliest countries for cryptocurrency and the blockchain technology. On September 29, 2017, the Swiss Financial Market Supervisory Authority (FINMA) published a directive[21] stating that it welcomes and recognizes the dynamic market of ICOs that have then been in high demand. They also recognized that there was no regulatory framework for ICOs, neither in Switzerland nor at international level, and that ICOs did not seem to violate any of the existing supervisory arrangements while some of them were likely to be covered by the existing laws.

A few months later, on February 16, 2018, FINMA published new guide-lines[22] to complement its previous directive, where the focus was shifted to the purpose of issuing the tokens, rather than a legal analysis.

FINMA categorized tokens into the following three types, recognizing possible hybrid forms:

i   *Payment tokens*: used as a means of payment for the acquisition of goods or as a medium of transfer of value;
ii *Utility tokens*: designed to give their owner digital access to an application or service;
iii *Asset tokens*: treated as assets that can bring future profits, in other words, similar to shares, bonds and derivatives.

The approach and the style of this directive clearly showed a positive attitude and interest of FINMA on the crypto-market.

6.9 Japan

Japan has so far maintained a positive position in the cryptocurrency industry having already set up a framework that makes it legal to use cryptocurrencies for payment purposes. Japan's approach to the ecosystem of cryptocurrencies has so far attracted several ICOs in the country, especially after the Chinese government banned ICOs, when many startups headed to Japan.

On October 27, 2017, the Financial Services Agency of Japan (FSA), the authority in charge of banking and insurance supervision, issued a press release[23] warning investors about the risks of ICOs. The two main risks highlighted were excess price volatility and the risk of potential fraud. The warning also mentioned that investors deal at their own risk and should invest only after understanding enough the risks and the content of an ICO project. It also stated that, depending on how ICOs are structured, they may fall under already existing regulation, such as the Payments Service Act and the Financial Instruments and Exchange Act and in this case, tokens issuers are required to comply with the above laws. Finally, they advised startups that conduct ICOs to fully comply with legal requirements, otherwise they could be prosecuted.

At the end of 2018, The Japan Cryptocurrency Business Association (JCBA) launched an ICO working group to develop appropriate ICO laws and regulations, an initiative that was welcomed by the Japanese regulatory authorities. On March 8, 2019, JCBA released their "Recommendations on New ICO Regulations"[24] focusing on how the domestic exchanges in Japan could be expanded to include cryptocurrencies. Regarding the ICO tokens, JCBA stated that

> Given that ICO tokens can promote Japan's industrial development in the future as a new financing method, it is not desirable to impose extremely strict regulations on those with a low risk from the perspective of user protection, which would make it virtually impossible to conduct ICOs.

76 The regulatory framework

Last, JCBA pointed out that the existing regulations lack balance, as they fail to take account the particularities of noninvestment ICOs. For this reason, they suggested separate regulations for utility tokens, since, contrary to security tokens, they serve as a means of settlement.

As for stablecoins, the regulatory framework still (Summer 2019) remains unclear in Japan and JCBA suggests that these should also be classified as cryptocurrencies, since stablecoins use the same technology as cryptocurrencies and they are mainly traded on cryptocurrency exchanges as well.

6.10 European Union (EU)

ICOs are allowed in the EU, provided that anti–money laundering policies are respected, that each ICO operation plan complies with the required business regulations, and that the respective licenses are granted. In this context, the European Securities and Markets Authority (ESMA) published (November 13, 2017) two statements regarding the ICOs – one for investors and one for companies.

As regards investors,[25] ESMA characterized ICOs as highly speculative investments, highlighting the following features. First there is a high risk of capital loss, due to high token price volatility. Second, most ICOs are not so far covered by any regulatory framework, which leaves investors unprotected in case of fraud. Third, the technology on which ICOs are based is still at an early stage and there is a high possibility that problems may appear. Last, the information that investors rely upon in order to invest cannot be officially controlled, and therefore investors can be misled.

As regards companies,[26] ESMA stated that the structure of the ICO will determine whether it falls within the EU regulatory framework or not. In case the tokens created by the ICO are transferable securities, the ICO must then comply with the EU regulatory requirements. That is, the company must publish an approved prospectus for the offer of transferable securities to the public and must receive the respective licenses. Also, under the 4th Anti-Money Laundering Directive, each company must have the necessary control systems and must take customer due diligence and continuous monitoring measures.

On January 9, 2019, the European Banking Authority (EBA)[27] and the European Securities and Markets Authority (ESMA)[28] published two reports providing advice on crypto-assets for the European Commission (EC), the EU Parliament, and the European Council. EBA mentioned that they monitor the progress of crypto-assets and analyze whether they fall under the Payment Services Directive 2 and the E-money Directive. They also noted that, due to the uncertainty regarding the implementation of the current Financial Services Act, each country approaches the issue differently. Finally, they advised on a continuous monitoring of crypto-assets as well as on their cost–benefit analysis as they expect rapid advancements in this area in the near future. The report ended with the following three main conclusions: (i) crypto-assets raise concerns regarding market integrity and consumer protection, (ii) most crypto-assets typically fall outside current EU financial services regulation, and (iii) crypto-assets activity in the EU is expected to increase. ESMA suggested that a special framework for crypto-assets that do not qualify as MiFID electronic money or financial instruments is created. They also stressed that such a framework should be tailored to the specific risks of crypto-assets and to the different requirements of each type. Both authorities concluded that when crypto-assets do not fall within the scope of EU financial services regulation, consumers are exposed to significant risks, and that all crypto-assets must be subject to anti-money laundering legislation.

6.11 Comparative analysis and conclusions of regulatory approaches

A common finding in all jurisdictions is that they all started regulating the ICO field after the summer of 2017. Until then, authorities were initially either indifferent, or reluctant, or even they were letting the industry grow and evolve by taking soft positions, from discussions or warnings (China, Japan) to official support (Switzerland, Singapore). During 2017, the crypto market ecosystem saw an explosion in both market values of cyptocurrencies and number of ICOs and respective funds raised, which prompted authorities to take action.

The first formal piece of regulation did not come until the July of 2017 where the US SEC issued the report for the DAO tokens, a step that might have worked as a signal to other authorities to follow with official regulatory decisions. All other jurisdictions followed the United States very quickly, issuing their legislation in just a couple of months after the United States.

Table 6.1 summarizes the different regulatory approaches discussed in the previous sections. All approaches can be categorized under the five following cases:

1. No position for ICOs
2. Active ICO and blockchain technology support
3. Active discussions and warnings
4. ICOs are regulated by the relevant legislation according to their nature
5. Prohibition of ICOs

Most regulatory authorities, based on the SEC interpretation, first explore whether digital tokens can be linked with financial securities, provided that the ICO structures that issue the tokens are such that these tokens share similar characteristics with financial securities. For example, the regulatory authorities of Canada, Australia, Singapore, and Japan are trying to regulate the ICOs via their existing rules on securities. This approach may be advantageous for investor protection purposes, but the real impact for the ICOs projects is still unclear since the regulatory burden is supposed to be relatively high in this case. For example, several ICOs in the United States either look to ensure that their tokens do not qualify as securities and therefore do not fall under SEC's regulations, or they are conducted in other countries and exclude US citizens for the same reason.

TABLE 6.1 Regulatory approaches of main jurisdictions

	2008–2015	2016	2017			2018–2019
			Jan–June	*July–Aug*	*Sept–Nov*	
UNITED STATES			----------			
SINGAPORE				----------		
CANADA						
CHINA – SOUTH KOREA		--------	----------	----------		
UNITED KINGDOM			----------	----------	----------	----------
AUSTRALIA				----------		
SWITZERLAND					----------	----------
JAPAN						
EUROPEAN UNION						

No position for ICOs
Active ICO support and Blockchain Technology
--------------Active discussions and warnings------------
ICOs regulated by the relevant legislation according to their nature
Prohibition of ICOs

The UK and Switzerland are to date the friendliest jurisdictions in terms of how they approach blockchain applications and the ICOs. These two countries differ from the group of countries discussed above in the sense that they have not strongly stated that their starting point is to explore whether tokens are financial assets; rather, they both introduce different categories of tokens, and thus leave it open on how these should be regulated.

European authorities have so far chosen to monitor how the industry evolves, without yet taking an official position on how to treat ICOs. There is no pan-European framework to cover all member states, and each state applies their own rules and approaches, based on the existing regulation that covers other areas of financial services. In this context, European projects that aim to conduct ICOs choose countries that have expressed a friendlier approach to ICOs (like Estonia, United Kingdom, and Switzerland), hoping that any forthcoming regulation will entail relatively few restrictions. This creates certain problems in cases where the project is legally based in one country, but investors that back the projects come from many other European countries, so that it is unclear which rules apply if something goes wrong with the project. This is why ESMA suggests that a single and pan-European regulation of ICOs should exist, covering a broader range of blockchain technology applications in general.

Last, China and South Korea are, so far, skeptical about the whole process of ICOs and have chosen to ban them. Both countries issued a ban on ICOs in September 2017 and the ban remains active to date (summer of 2019), even though there are currently discussions of possibly lifting the ban in South Korea.

Notes

1 Securities and Exchange Commission. (2017). "Report of Investigation Pursuant to Section (21a) of the Securities Exchange Act of 1934: The DAO" (July 25). Available at: www.sec.gov/litigation/investreport/34-81207.pdf.
2 The DAO (Decentralized Autonomous Organization) was a project designed on the Ethereum platform, which aimed to raise funds from investors by using smart contract technology. It then invested the raised funds in other projects. It was like a decentralized venture capital fund. From April to June 2017, DAO raised funds of $150 million. A few days later, a loophole was discovered in the code of the DAO network and lots of funds were transferred by hacker(s). This triggered SEC investigation that led to the respective report and press release.
3 Securities and Exchange Commission. (2017). "U.S. Securities Laws May Apply to Offers, Sales, and Trading of Interests in Virtual Organizations" (July 25). Available at: www.sec.gov/news/press-release/2017-131.
4 www.sec.gov/news/press-release/2017-176.
5 www.sec.gov/ICO.
6 Funderbeam, (2017): Initial Coin Offering funding report. Available at: https://coinreport.net/wp-content/uploads/2017/12/Funderbeam-report.pdf.
7 Monetary Authority of Singapore (MAS). (2017). "Consumer Advisory on Investment Schemes Involving Digital Tokens (Including Virtual Currencies)" (10 August). Available at: www.mas.gov.sg/News-and-Publications/Media-Releases/2017/Consumer-Advisory-on-Investment-Schemes-Involving-Digital-Tokens.aspx.
8 Monetary Authority of Singapore (MAS). (2017). "A guide to Digital Token Offerings" (November 14).
9 Monetary Authority of Singapore (MAS). (2019). "A guide to Digital Token Offerings" (April 5).
10 The regulatory sandbox environment is a protective regulatory environment where the regulatory requirements are more relaxed, so that the project owners can test their business plans, while the authorities can monitor the project and develop better understanding of the structure of the ICO.
11 Canadian Securities Administrators (2017), CSA Staff Notice 46–307 – "Cryptocurrency Offerings" (August 24). Available at: www.osc.gov.on.ca/en/SecuritiesLaw_csa_20170824_cryptocurrency-offerings.htm.
12 Canadian Securities Administrators (CSA) and Investment Industry Regulatory Organization of Canada (IIROC). (2009). "Joint CSA/IIROC Consultation Paper 21-402 Proposed Framework for CryptoAsset Trading Platforms" (March 14). Available at: www.securities-administrators.ca/aboutcsa.aspx?id=1776.
13 The People's Bank of China. (2017). "Public Notice of the PBC, CAC, MIIT, SAIC, CBRC, CSRC, and CIRC on Preventing Risks of Fundraising through Coin Offering" (September 4). Available at: www.pbc.gov.cn/english/130721/3377816/index.html.
14 Financial Services Commission of South Korea (FSC). (2017). "Joint TF of Virtual Currency Related Organizations is held to check the progress of each organization" (Press Release, September). Available at: www.fsc.go.kr/info/ntc_news_view.jsp?bbsid=BBS0030&page=1&sch1=&sword=&r_url=&menu=7210100&no=32085.
15 FCA. (2017). "Discussion Paper on Distributed Ledger Technology" (DP 17/3, April). Available at: www.fca.org.uk/publication/discussion/dp17-03.pdf.
16 FCA. (2017). "Consumer Warning about the Risks of Initial Coin Offerings (ICOs)" (September 12). Available at: www.fca.org.uk/news/statements/initial-coin-offerings.

80 The regulatory framework

17 Cryptoassets Taskforce: Final Report, (October 2018), Available at: https://assets.publishing.service.gov.uk/government/uploads/system/uploads/attachment_data/file/752070/cryptoassets_taskforce_final_report_final_web.pdf.
18 Financial Conduct Authority (FCA). (2019). "Guidance on Cryptoassets." Consultation Paper CP19/3, (January), Available at: www.fca.org.uk/publication/consultation/cp19-03.pdf.
19 Australian Securities & Investments Commission. (2017). "Initial Coin Offerings, Information sheet 225." Available at: http://asic.gov.au/regulatory-resources/digital-transformation/initial-coin-offerings/.
20 Australian Government, "Enhanced Regulatory Sandbox." Available at: https://treasury.gov.au/consultation/c2017-t230052/.
21 FINMA (Financial Market Supervisory Authority). (2017). "FINMA is Investigating ICO Procedures" (September 29). Available at: www.finma.ch/en/news/2017/09/20170929-mm-ico/.
22 FINMA (Financial Market Supervisory Authority). (2017). "FINMA is Publishes ICO Guidelines" (February 16). Available at www.finma.ch/en/news/2018/02/20180216-mm-ico-wegleitung/.
23 Japan Financial Services Agency. (2017). Initial Coin Offerings (ICOs) – "User and Business Operator Warning about the Risks of ICOs" (October 27). Available at: www.fsa.go.jp/policy/virtual_currency/07.pdf.
24 Japan Cryptocurrency Business Association (JCBA). (2019). "Recommendations on New ICO Regulations" (March 8). Available at: https://cryptocurrency-association.org/news/main-info/20190308-001/.
25 European Securities & Markets Authority. (2017). "Statement: ESMA alerts investors to the high risks of Initial Coin Offerings (ICOs)." (November 13). Available at: www.esma.europa.eu/sites/default/files/library/esma50-157- 829_ico_statement_investors.pdf.
26 European Securities & Markets Authority. (2017). "Statement: ESMA alerts firms involved in Initial Coin Offerings (ICOs) to the need to meet relevant regulatory requirements" (November 13). Available at: www.esma.europa.eu/sites/default/files/library/esma50-157- 828_ico_statement_firms.pdf.
27 European Banking Authority (EBA) (2019). "Report on Crypto Assets with advice for the European Commission" (January 9). Available at: https://eba.europa.eu/documents/10180/2545547/EBA+Report+on+crypto+assets.pdf.
28 European Securities & Markets Authority (ESMA). (2019). "Advice Initial Coin Offerings and Crypto-Assets" (January 9). Available at: www.esma.europa.eu/sites/default/files/library/esma50-157-1391_crypto_advice.pdf.

Bibliography

ASIC. "FS licensees." Available at: www.asic.gov.au/for-finance-professionals/afs-licensees/
Australian Government. "Federal Register of Legislation: Corporations Act 2001 (Cth)." Available at: www.legislation.gov.au/Series/C2004A00818
Australian Government. "Enhanced Regulatory Sandbox." Available at: https://treasury.gov.au/consultation/c2017-t230052/
Australian Securities and Investments Commission. (2017). "Initial Coin Offerings, Information Sheet 225." Available at: http://asic.gov.au/regulatory-resources/digital-transformation/initial-coin-offerings/
Barsan, Iris M. (2017). Legal Challenges of Initial Coin Offerings (ICO) (November 2). *Revue Trimestrielle de Droit Financier (RTDF)*, n° 3, pp. 54–65. Available at: SSRN: https://papers.ssrn.com/sol3/papers.cfm?abstract_id=3064397

The regulatory framework **81**

Canadian Securities Administrators. (2017). CSA Staff Notice 46-307 – "Cryptocurrency Offerings" (August 24). Available at: www.osc.gov.on.ca/en/SecuritiesLaw_csa_20170824_cryptocurrency-offerings.htm

Canadian Securities Administrators (CSA) & Investment Industry Regulatory Organization of Canada (IIROC). (2009). "Joint CSA/IIROC Consultation Paper 21-402 Proposed Framework for CryptoAsset Trading Platforms" (March 14). Available at: www.securities-administrators.ca/aboutcsa.aspx?id=1776

Clifford Chance. (2018). "Initial Coin Offerings – Asking the Right Regulatory Questions" (May). Available at: www.cliffordchance.com/briefings/2018/05/initial_coin_offeringsaskingtherigh.html

Cryptoassets Taskforce: Final Report. (2018, October). Available at: https://assets.publishing.service.gov.uk/government/uploads/system/uploads/attachment_data/file/752070/cryptoassets_taskforce_final_report_final_web.pdf

European Securities & Markets Authority. (2017). "Statement: ESMA alerts investors to the high risks of Initial Coin Offerings (ICOs)" (November 13). Available at: www.esma.europa.eu/sites/default/files/library/esma50-157- 829_ico_statement_investors.pdf

European Securities & Markets Authority. (2017). "Statement: ESMA alerts firms involved in Initial Coin Offerings (ICOs) to the need to meet relevant regulatory requirements" (November 13). Available at: www.esma.europa.eu/sites/default/files/library/esma50-157-828_ico_statement_firms.pdf

European Banking Authority (EBA). (2019). "Report on Crypto Assets with Advice for the European Commission" (January 9). Available at: https://eba.europa.eu/documents/10180/2545547/EBA+Report+on+crypto+assets.pdf

European Securities & Markets Authority (ESMA). (2019). "Advice Initial Coin Offerings and Crypto-Assets" (January 9). Available at: www.esma.europa.eu/sites/default/files/library/esma50-157-1391_crypto_advice.pdf

Financial Conduct Authority (FCA). (2017). "Discussion Paper on Distributed Ledger Technology" (DP 17/3, April). Available at: www.fca.org.uk/publication/discussion/dp17-03.pdf

Financial Conduct Authority (FCA). (2017). "Consumer Warning about the Risks of Initial Coin Offerings (ICOs)" (September 12). Available at: www.fca.org.uk/news/statements/initial-coin-offerings

Financial Conduct Authority (FCA). (2019). "Guidance on Cryptoassets." Consultation Paper CP19/3 (January). Available at: www.fca.org.uk/publication/consultation/cp19-03.pdf

Financial Services Commission of South Korea (FSC). (2017). "Joint TF of Virtual Currency Related Organizations is held to check the progress of each organization" (Press Release, September). Available at: www.fsc.go.kr/info/ntc_news_view.jsp?bbsid=BBS0030&page=1&sch1=&sword=&r_url=&menu=7210100&no=32085

FINMA (Financial Market Supervisory Authority). (2017a). "FINMA Is Investigating ICO Procedures" (September 29). Available at: www.finma.ch/en/news/2017/09/20170929-mm-ico/

FINMA (Financial Market Supervisory Authority). (2017b). "FINMA is Publishes ICO Guidelines" (February 16). Available at: www.finma.ch/en/news/2018/02/20180216-mm-ico-wegleitung/

Funderbeam. (2017). "Initial Coin Offering Funding Report." Available at: https://coinreport.net/wp-content/uploads/2017/12/Funderbeam-report.pdf

82 The regulatory framework

Japan Cryptocurrency Business Association (JCBA). (2019). "Recommendations on New ICO Regulations" (March 8). Available at: https://cryptocurrency-association.org/news/main-info/20190308-001/

Japan Financial Services Agency. (2017). "Initial Coin Offerings (ICOs) – User and Business Operator Warning about the Risks of ICOs" (October 27). Available at: www.fsa.go.jp/policy/virtual_currency/07.pdf

Karsten, Wockener, Carsten, Losing, Thilo, Diehl, and Annekatrin, Kutzbach. (2017). "Regulation of Initial Coin Offerings" (December). *White & Case*. Available at: www.whitecase.com/publications/alert/regulation-initial-coin-offerings

Monetary Authority of Singapore (MAS). (2017). "Consumer Advisory on Investment Schemes Involving Digital Tokens (Including Virtual Currencies)" (August 10). Available at: www.mas.gov.sg/News-and-Publications/Media-Releases/2017/Consumer-Advisory-on-Investment-Schemes-Involving-Digital-Tokens.aspx

Monetary Authority of Singapore (MAS). (2017). "A Guide to Digital Token Offerings" (November 14). Available at: www.mas.gov.sg/News-and-Publications/Monographs-and-Information-Papers/2017/Guidance-on-Digital-Token-Offerings.aspx

Monetary Authority of Singapore (MAS). (2019). "A Guide to Digital Token Offerings" (November 5). Available at: www.mas.gov.sg/News-and-Publications/Monographs-and-Information-Papers/2019/A-Guide-to-Digital-Token-Offerings.aspx

Quek Li Fei. (2017). "How Initial Coin Offerings ('ICOs') are Regarded or Regulated in Various Countries" (December). *cnplaw*. Available at: www.cnplaw.com/how-initial-coin-offerings-icos-are-regarded-or-regulated-in-various-countries/

Securities and Exchange Commission. (2017). "Report of Investigation Pursuant to Section (21a) of the Securities Exchange Act of 1934: The DAO" (July 25). Available at: www.sec.gov/litigation/investreport/34-81207.pdf

Securities and Exchange Commission. (2017). "SEC Announces Enforcement Initiatives to Combat Cyber-Based Threats and Protect Retail Investors" (September 25). Available at: www.sec.gov/news/press-release/2017-176

Securities and Exchange Commission. (2017). "U.S. Securities Laws May Apply to Offers, Sales, and Trading of Interests in Virtual Organizations" (July 25). Available at: www.sec.gov/news/press-release/2017-131

Stephenson Harwood. (2018). "Initial Coin Offerings and Regulation – A Review of Significant Jurisdictions." Briefing Note (February). Available at: www.shlegal.com/docs/default-source/news-insights-documents/02-18-stephenson-harwood-initial-coin-offerings-and-regulation.pdf?sfvrsn=2a5f105b_0

Takaharu, Totsuka, Ken, Kawai, and Takato, Fukui. (2017). "Initial Coin Offering" November. *Financial Services & Transactions Group Newsletter, Anderson Mori & Tomotsune*. Available at: www.amt-law.com/asset/pdf/bulletins2_pdf/171101.pdf

The People's Bank of China. (2017). "Public Notice of the PBC, CAC, MIIT, SAIC, CBRC, CSRC and CIRC on Preventing Risks of Fundraising through Coin Offering" (September 4). Available at: www.pbc.gov.cn/english/130721/3377816/index.html

INDEX

Note: **Bold** page numbers refer to tables; *italic* page numbers refer to figures and page numbers followed by "n" denote endnotes.

AirDrops 59
altcoins (alternative cryptocurrencies) 28, 29, 51
AML *see* anti-money laundering (AML)
anonymity 27
anti-money laundering (AML) 18, 72, 76
ASIC *see* Australian Securities and Investment Committee (ASIC)
"asset tokens" 37, 75
auction-type process 33
Australia 74
Australian Securities and Investment Committee (ASIC) 74

Babylonian records 5
Bank for International Settlements (BIS) 21, 24
Bank of England 73
"beat the market" 52
Big Data 17
BIS *see* Bank for International Settlement (BIS)
Bitcoin 3, 9, 28, 33, 53, 69; *see also* blockchain technology; cryptocurrency
"Bitcoin: A Peer-to-Peer Electronic Cash System" (Nakamoto) 3
bitcoin price 28–29
"Bit Gold" 3
Blockchain 2.0 15–16

blockchain technology: annual energy consumption 12; applications of 17–18; bitcoin network 56; centralized systems 10, *10*; consensus mechanisms 13–15; cryptography method 4; decentralized systems 10, *10*; definition of 9–10; distributed system 10, *10*; encrypted digital information 11; "encrypted finance," notion of 4; EOS cryptocurrencies 14; initial coin offerings 55; "mining" process 12–13; new era of encrypted finance 3–5; peer-to-peer electronic cash system 3, 6; peer-to-peer payment system 9; record-keeping service of 12; safety 26–27; safety, transparency, and irreversibility 11–12; "smart contracts" 16–17; as spreadsheet 9; works, transaction in 11, *11*
"B-money" 3
BTC-USD price fluctuations *48*, 50
Buterin, Vitalik 15

Canada 72
Canadian Securities Administrators (CSA) 72
capital asset pricing model (CAPM) 44
capital markets product 71
CAPM *see* capital asset pricing model (CAPM)
Caporale, Guglielmo Maria 53

84 Index

centralized systems 10, *10*
CFT *see* Countering Financing of Terrorism (CFT)
Chaum, David 3
China 31, 72–73
"commodities" 32, 44, 72
consensus mechanisms: delegated proof of stake 14; proof of burn 15; proof of elapsed time 14–15; proof of importance 15; proof of space/capacity 14; proof of stake 13; proof of work 13
consumer protection 8, 76
convertibility 27
cost–benefit analysis 76
Countering Financing of Terrorism (CFT) 72
crowdfunding 7, 20, 64–66, **66**
crowd sale step 59–60
crypto-assets 7, 72, 73, 76–77
Cryptoassets Task Force 73
crypto-collateralized stablecoins 33
cryptocurrency 9, 23–24; advertisements 29; alternative cryptocurrencies 28; anonymity 27; convertibility 27; crypto market *28*, 28–31, *29*, *30*; decentralization 26; definition of 23–24; finite supply 27; irreversibility 27; safety 26–27; stablecoins 31–34, *32*, **34**; transactions work 24–26; transparency 27
cryptocurrency ecosystem: initial coin offerings 56–58
cryptocurrency transactions 12
cryptographic hash functions 4
cryptographic methods 4, 10
crypto markets 7, 8, *28*, 28–31, *29*, **30**, 77; discounted cash flow (DCF) model 43–44
CSA *see* Canadian Securities Administrators (CSA)
"currency", types of 31, 62; cryptocurrencies 23–24; digital currencies 21–22; tokens 24; virtual currencies 22–23
"currency" concept 24
Cyber Unit 70

Dai, Wei 3
DAO *see* decentralized autonomous organization (DAO)
DCF model *see* discounted cash flow (DCF) model
decentralization 26
decentralized autonomous organization (DAO) 70, 79n2
decentralized systems 10, *10*

decision-making process 45
delegated proof of stake (DPoS) 14
"descending triangle" 47
diagrammatic analysis: geometrical patterns 47; line/bar charts 46–47
digital asset 3, 31
digital currency 3, 21–22; assets, digital form 21–22; definition of 21; digital payment mechanism 21
digital payment mechanism 9, 21
digital signatures 4, 27
digital wallet 23, 25, *25*
discounted cash flow (DCF) model 43–44
"distributed ledgers" system 4
distributed ledger technology (DLT) 10, 70, 73
distributed system 10, *10*
DLT *see* distributed ledger technology (DLT)
donation- and rewards-based crowdfunding 62
double-spending problem 3, 4, 9
DPoS *see* delegated proof of stake (DPoS)

"eater address" 15
EBA *see* European Banking Authority (EBA)
EC *see* European Commission (EC)
ECB *see* European Central Bank (ECB)
economic perspective 7
efficient market hypothesis (EMH) 52, *52*
EMA *see* exponential moving average (EMA)
"e-money" 21
E-money Directive 76
encrypted finance: blockchain technology 4; double-spending problem 3, 4
ENISA *see* European Union Agency for Cybersecurity (ENISA)
EOS cryptocurrency project 14
escrow-based milestones 60
ESMA *see* European Securities and Markets Authority (ESMA)
Ethereum platform 6, 15–16
European Banking Authority (EBA) 23, 34n10, 76
European Central Bank (ECB) 22, 34n9
European Commission (EC) 76
European Securities and Markets Authority (ESMA) 24, 76–78
European Union 76–77
European Union Agency for Cybersecurity (ENISA) 24
exchange tokens 74
exponential moving average (EMA) 47

Index **85**

fair lottery system 14
FATF *see* Financial Action Task Force (FATF)
FCA *see* Financial Conduct Authority (FCA)
Federal Securities Law 70
fiat-collateralized stablecoins 31–32
fiat currency 31
Financial Action Task Force (FATF) 21, 22, 24, 34n2
Financial Conduct Authority (FCA) 73, 74
financial infrastructure: circulatory system of 3; financial intermediaries (indirect finance) 1, 2; financial markets (direct finance) 1, 2; functions of 2–3
financial institutions 3–4
financial intermediaries (indirect finance) 1, 2
financial markets (direct finance) 1, 2
financial middleman 5
Financial Services Act 76
Financial Services Agency of Japan (FSA) 75
Financial Stability Committee (FSC) 73
"financial system": basic functions of 2; definition of 1; financial infrastructure 1, 2; market-based economy 2; middlemen in 5; payment system 2–3; trust, notion of 2
finite supply, cryptocurrencies 27
FINMA *see* Swiss Financial Market Supervisory Authority (FINMA)
First bitcoin transaction *4*
"5 things to know," US Securities and Exchange Commission 70–71
4th Anti-Money Laundering Directive 76
FSA *see* Financial Services Agency of Japan (FSA)
FSC *see* Financial Stability Committee (FSC)
funder receives, type of 62

Genesis Block in Bitcoin 3
geometrical patterns, price trends: BTC-USD price fluctuations *48*; continuation patterns 47; reversal patterns 47
Global Financial Crisis 2008 2, 7
Gnosis project 57
"Guide to Digital Token Offerings" 71

hard-mining process 13
HM Treasury 73

ICOs *see* initial coin offerings (ICOs)
IIROC *see* Investment Industry Regulatory Organization of Canada (IIROC)

IMF *see* International Monetary Fund (IMF)
indicators and oscillators tool 47–51
initial coin offerings (ICOs) 7, 8, 40, 42; crowdfunding 64–66, **66**; crowd sale step 59–60; cryptocurrency ecosystem 56–58; definition of 55–56; development of 56–57; dynamic market of 74; features of 61; initial public offerings 63–64, **65**; offer step 59; participants in *56*; PR campaign step 59; pre-announcement step 58; regulatory framework 61, 69; tokens 61–62; *vs.* venture capital 56, *57*; white paper, importance of 62–63
initial public offering (IPO) 7, 63–64, **65**
International Monetary Fund (IMF) 20, *21*, 22
Investment Industry Regulatory Organization of Canada (IIROC) 72
investment scheme 71
investors behavior 45
investors risk 73
IPO *see* initial public offering (IPO)
irreversibility 27

Japan 75–76
Japan Cryptocurrency Business Association (JCBA) 75, 76

know your customer (KYC) 18
Kristoufek, L. 53
KYC *see* know your customer (KYC)

Larimer, Daniel 14
Latif, S. R. 53
ledger 4, 5, 9–11, 13, 70
linear regression approach 50–51
Litecoin 29, 53
London Stock Exchange (LSE) 1, 6

MACD *see* moving average convergence/divergence (MACD)
magnitude of price changes 50
market-based economy 2
market discounts 45
market participants 38
market psychology 44
MAS *see* Monetary Authority of Singapore (MAS)
Mastercoin 56
mathematical-statistical analysis: indicators and oscillators 47–51; linear regression approach 50–51; market psychology 44
middlemen 5
MiFID electronic money 77

86 Index

miners 12–15
"mining" process 12, 14, 18n2
Monetary Authority of Singapore (MAS) 71, 72, 79n7
monetary policy 33, 40, 42–43, *43*
moving average convergence/divergence (MACD) 47–49, *49*

Nakamoto, Satoshi 3; "Bitcoin: A Peer-to-Peer Electronic Cash System" 3; blockchain technology 4, 9–10; cryptocurrency idea 4; Genesis Block in Bitcoin 3
NEM cryptocurrency project 15
new encrypted financial system: fundraising 7; infrastructure 5; regulation 7–8; "tokenomics" and valuation 6–7; traded assets 6
nodes 9–15, 27
noncollateralized stablecoins 33–34

offer step 59
"Open-high-low-close" (OHLC) 45–46
"over-collateralization" process 33

pan-European framework 78
past market activity 45
Payment Services Directive 2 76
payments infrastructure 5
payment system 2–3; functions of 2–3
payment tokens 75
peer-to-peer electronic cash system 3, 6, 9
percentage price oscillator (PPO) 49, *50*
PoB *see* proof of burn (PoB)
PoET *see* proof of elapsed time (PoET)
PoI *see* proof of importance (PoI)
PoS *see* proof of stake (PoS)
potential fraud, risk of 75
PoW *see* proof of work (PoW)
PPO *see* percentage price oscillator (PPO)
PR campaign step 59
pre-announcement step 58
price and volume trends 45
price determination model 38
price fluctuations 46
price volatility 75, 76
pricing and valuation models 37
private key 25–26, *25*
progressive banking regulations 74
project, integral part of 62
proof of burn (PoB) 15
proof of elapsed time (PoET) 14–15
proof of importance (PoI) 15
proof of space/capacity mechanism 14
proof of stake (PoS) 13, 14

proof of work (PoW) 13, 14
public address 25
public key 25–26, *25*

quantitative theory of money 40–42; application of 42; crypto market ecosystem 41–43; exchange, equation of 41

"Recommendations on New ICO Regulations" 75
regulatory approaches 77, **78**
regulatory framework: Australia 74; Canada 72; China 72–73; European Union 76–77; Japan 75–76; Singapore 71–72; South Korea 72–73; Switzerland 74–75; United Kingdom 73–74; United States 70–71
regulatory sandbox scheme 72, 79n10
relative strength index (RSI) 49–50, *51*

safety 26–27
seasoned equity offerings (SEOs) 7
SEC *see* US Securities and Exchange Commission (SEC)
Securities Act 72
Securities and Futures Act (SFA) 71
"security tokens" 37, 74
SEOs *see* seasoned equity offerings (SEOs)
SFA *see* Securities and Futures Act (SFA)
sharing economy 18
Singapore 71–72
Singaporean securities laws 71
"smart contracts" 16–17
South Korea 31, 72–73
stablecoins 6, 31–34, *32*, **34**; advantages of 33; crypto-collateralized stablecoins 33; fiat-collateralized stablecoins 31–32; noncollateralized stablecoins 33–34
supply and demand model 38–40, *39*
Swiss Financial Market Supervisory Authority (FINMA) 74, 75
Switzerland 74–75
"systemic risk" 2, 3
Szabo, Nick 3, 16, 18n3

technical analysis, crypto market: advantage of 51; assumptions of 45; diagrammatic analysis 45; efficient market hypothesis 51–53; mathematical-statistical analysis 45; past market activity 45
"token burn" 40
token buyback 40
token distribution 40, 58
token monetary policy approach 38–40

"tokenomics" and valuation *see* tokens; valuation model

tokens 24; buyback strategy 40; "fair" value of 37; financial assets 6–7; initial coin offerings 61–62; monetary policies 42–43; pricing and valuation 37–38; quantitative theory of money 40–42; supply and demand model 38–40, *39*; transactions, volume and speed of 41; utility, economics of 42–43

tourism industry 17

traditional financial assets 6, 7

traditional financial system 1–3; basics of 3; blockchain technology 5; financial infrastructure 1–2, *2*; payment system 2–3

traditional valuation methods 37

transactions services 2–9, 12–18, 31, 41, 62, 73

transactions work 24–26

transparency 27

"true" function 38, 42

trust, notion of 2, 3

United Kingdom 73–74

United States 70–71, 77

US dollar/bitcoin (USD/BTC) price fluctuation 46, *46, 48*

US Securities and Exchange Commission (SEC) 70, 71

US Treasury Department (FinCEN) 23, 34n11

utility, economics of 42–43, *43*

utility tokens 74, 75

valuation, financial assets 6–7

valuation model: crypto market, technical analysis 44–45; discounted cash flow (DCF) model 43–44; monetary policies 42–43; quantity theory of money 40–42; token supply and demand model 38–40; utility, token economics of 42–43

venture capital (VC) 56, *57*

virtual currencies: definition of 22, 23; ECB classification of 22–23

virtual mining right 15

Vosvrda, M. 53

weighted average cost of capital (WACC) 44

white paper, importance of 58, 62–63

World Bank 21, 24